Body Parts

Sticking Place Books 2026
© Alex Cox and Rudy Wurlitzer
Introduction © James Kenney

Cover photographs © Lynn Davis

www.stickingplacebooks.com

ISBN 979-8-89976-081-5

Body Parts

Alex Cox
and
Rudy Wurlitzer

Sticking Place Books
New York

Zero
Tolerance

Sticking Place Books 2026
© Alex Cox and Rudy Wurlitzer
Introduction © James Kenney

Cover photographs © Lynn Davis.

www.stickingplacebooks.com

ISBN 979-8-89976-081-5

Zero Tolerance

Alex Cox
and
Rudy Wurlitzer

Sticking Place Books
New York

Cox/Wurlitzer 2: *Zero Tolerance*
by James Kenney

John Hull was hard to pin down. Which suited John Hull just fine.

Hull was an American rancher who had made himself at home in Costa Rica, acquired citizenship, and spent the years from 1982 through 1986 running Contra supply operations from his ranch near the Nicaraguan border. Or so Costa Rican authorities would eventually allege, to remarkably little consequence.

Hull had also, according to Colombian drug kingpin Carlos Lehder, been pumping roughly thirty tons of cocaine a year into the United States.

When Hull's role surfaced during the Iran-Contra investigation as having been working for both the C.I.A. and the Oliver North network, serving as liaison between Americans and Contra groups on the "Southern Front," Alex Cox took notice and shared what he had gathered with Rudy Wurlitzer. They made a trip to Washington together to meet one of the Iran-Contra investigators and, as Cox puts it, "complain to our representatives."

What particularly interested Cox was the La Penca bombing of May 1984, in which an explosive was detonated at a press conference in Nicaragua while moderate Contra commander Edén Pastora was meeting with reporters. It killed five people, including three journalists, and wounding a dozen more. Costa Rica would eventually charge Hull with engineering the action. In July 1989, facing drug trafficking and murder charges, Hull skipped bail and fled to the United States, where he lived on his farm in Indiana, made occasional trips to Central America, and was never extradited. The machinery, as it tends to do, held firm. Cox and Wurlitzer meanwhile, wrote *Zero Tolerance*.

The film they envisioned was a political thriller with genre bones. Cox had been circling this territory since *Walker*—his portrait of William Walker, the nineteenth-century American mercenary who invaded Nicaragua and briefly crowned himself president, a film made precisely because the parallel to Reagan's Central America was too conspicuous for Cox to ignore. Hull was not a historical figure. He was alive, living on a farm, and nobody was coming for him. Where *Walker* worked through the distance of history, *Zero Tolerance* wanted to close that gap entirely.

For the lead role of Sam Gundy, Cox and Wurlitzer wanted Dennis Hopper. "He was up for it," Cox recalls, "but his agent said no. And actors must do as their agents say." Richard Gere was also considered, attached at one point to play the CIA operative Worth Bigelow. Cox remembers having dinner with Gere in New York, where the actor spoke with genuine enthusiasm about Wurlitzer's writing, telling friends, "Rudy's script contains the Four Noble Truths of Buddhism!" Cox adds the deflating coda: "He was referring to *Zebulon*, another Wurlitzer script. And he didn't do that one, either."

Zero Tolerance was radioactive in precisely the way the industry least tolerates. It was compelling, had its share of action and intrigue, but demanded that audiences know something, or at least be willing to learn, and be confronted with a narrative climax that offered no comfortable resolution. Which is precisely what makes the screenplay worth our attention today. The Iran-Contra affair has long since been absorbed into the fog of recent history. A scandal that burned briefly, then was managed, then was mostly forgotten. What Cox and Wurlitzer built in response was not a documentary impulse dressed in thriller clothing but something harder to dismiss: a screenplay that understood how power actually operates. Through proxies, through plausible deniability, through the exploitation of institutions too compromised or too incurious to look closely, Wurlitzer's gift for philosophical weight and Cox's instinct for political outrage found in *Zero Tolerance* a subject that demanded both at once.

"No one would make a film with the commies who made *Walker*," Cox later observed. The remark is characteristic of him: dry, accurate, delivered without self-pity. History has certainly vindicated Cox and Wurlitzer. The world *Zero Tolerance* describes—its mechanisms, its impunity, its contempt for accountability—did not go away. It metastasized.

BY ALEX COX &
RUDY WURLITZER

©1988
The Together Brothers

<u>ARIZONA DESERT</u> EXT NIGHT

BEFORE DAWN.

NICK CUZCO rides his three-wheeled AMC Desert Ghost Mk III
across the desert floor.

He speeds up a triangular, flat-topped mesa.

He pulls up just before the cliff.

NICK wears the uniform of Cactus Security Systems.
Its logo, three saguaro cactus with a padlock around them.,
is emblazoned on his right sleeve and his tricycle.

He takes off his full-face helmet and reaches for his cigarettes.

NICK is in his late twenties. Sandy hair and Wyatt Earp moustache.

A COMET APPEARS OVERHEAD.

THE COMET TRACES A ZIG-ZAG PATTERN ACROSS THE SKY.

IT EXPLODES IN A TRIANGULAR CLUSTER OF STARS.

NICK watches in amazement.

Something moves on the desert floor, beneath him.
The tail lights of a pickup truck creeping across the plain.

<u>DESERT</u> EXT DAWN

A forest of tall saguaro cactus.

The CAMACHO BROTHERS – BENNY, PACO and FREDDY - are poaching
cactus in the silent dawn.

Digging them up with shovels, they throw them in the back of their
pickup truck.

BENNY pops open three beers in celebration of the night's catch -
a dozen prime saguaro cactus destined for lawyers' offices and banks
in Phoenix.

FREDDY loads firewood on top of the ILLEGAL HAUL.

WHRRRR.

The whine of a charged-up AMC Desert Ghost is heard.

The BROTHERS CAMACHO make a fast move for the truck.

Too late. NICK CUZCO appears, sailing over a dune on his high-velocity three-wheeler.

NICK dismounts, unholstering his .38 special and CITATION BOOK.

                    NICK
          You assholes. I'm gonna have
          to take you in.

                    BENNY
          Don't be a hard-on, Nick.
          We'll put 'em back.

                    PACO
          No we won't.

                    NICK
          Sorry, boys, I need the bust.

                    BENNY
          What you going for, promotion?

                    NICK
              (taking out handcuffs)
          Turn around.

                    BENNY
          Cabron.

                    FREDDY
          You ain't never gonna get promotion.

                    NICK
          You turn around too, Freddy. Don't even
          think of giving me a hard time.

A SMALL PLANE flies low overhead.

                    BENNY
          Fuck you, Nick! You should be helping us
          dig 'em up. Or else busting SKY KINGS
          like that dude up there!

                    FREDDY
          Yeah! Bust the DRUG SMUGGLERS, not
          the guys from your own neighborhood.

                    NICK
          For the last time, turn around.

                    BENNY
          What if we don't do it for you, Nick?
          What you going to do about that?

                    NICK
          You'll find out.

No one moves. In the distance, the PLANE lands.

                    PACO
          Big time CACTUS RUSTLERS, Nick!

NICK jumps up on the cab of the CAMACHO BROTHERS' truck.
He pulls out his binoculars.

                    FREDDY
          Get off our truck, man!

NICK'S POV – THE PLANE HAS LANDED IN A DRY LAKE BED.
IT TAXIS TO A HALT.   NICK lowers the binoculars.

                    NICK
               Let's go.

                    BENNY
               Go where?

                    NICK
          Check out that plane.

                    BENNY
          No, man. I'm not going near that plane.
          Those dope guys are crazy. They're
          bad dudes.

LOW, HEROIC ANGLE ON NICK.

                    NICK
          They may have engine trouble, Benny.
          They may be in serious difficulties.
          We'll settle our account later.

Right now, follow me.

                    BENNY
          Whatever you say, *jefe.*

NICK nods and strides towards his three-wheeler.

The CAMACHO BROTHERS head for their pickup.

They follow NICK until he tops a rise.

As soon as he is out of sight, they turn around and head the other way.

DRY LAKE BED   EXT   MORNING

NICK speeds across the LAKE BED towards the AIRPLANE.
His head is down.

A MAN stands beside the plane, smoking a cigarette.
He is a heavy-set German, wearing a Yankee baseball cap. THORNTON.

NICK stops twenty feet away. His dust cloud catches up with him.
It clears. THORNTON hasn't moved.

                    NICK
          Are you all right?

                    THORNTON
          Yeah, I'm all right. How are you?

NICK looks past THORNTON at TWO BOXES lying beneath the plane.

Written on the side of the plane are the words,

          LONGHORN AIR TRANSPORT

                    NICK
          I thought you might have crashed or had
          fuel problems. Where you coming from?

                    THORNTON
          Phoenix.

                    NICK
          That's funny. I thought you were coming
          from the South. What's in the Boxes?

NICK puts his hand on the butt on his gun.

                    THORNTON
          I can't hear you.

NICK tugs at the chin strap of his helmet.

                    NICK
          I said, WHAT'S IN THE BOXES?

                    THORNTON
          Frozen shrimp.

A TRUCK is approaching.

                    NICK
          I'd like to take a look inside, if you
          don't mind.

NICK takes his helmet off.

THORNTON kicks NICK in the balls.

NICK topples forward, dropping his helmet, grabbing for his gun.

THORNTON whacks NICK with his CRASH HELMET.

NICK BLACKS OUT.

DESERT   EXT   LATER THAT DAY

NICK WAKES UP.

He sees many sets of POLISHED BOOTS.

The boots belong to ALL KINDS OF POLICE OFFICERS – TUCSON DETECTIVES, STATE TROOPERS, D.E.A., F.B.I., BORDER PATROL – all prowling around the EMPTY SITE picking up cigarette butts and making plaster casts.

THE PLANE AND TRUCK ARE GONE.

MANY COPS gather round NICK as he wakes.

                    NICK
          Did you get 'em?

                    COP 1

No, we didn't. Thanks to you.

                    NICK
          What do you mean? I –

He grabs his bruised head in pain.

                    COP 2
          You just fucked up the biggest bust
          in Arizona history.

POLICE STATION   INT   NIGHT

NICK receives the third degree. He sits on a stool under a bright light.
SEVERAL COPS interrogate him.

                    COP 3
          You were waiting for them, weren't
          you, Cuzco? What happened?
          Did they double cross you?

                    NICK
          You guys are mad at me because I was
          the first man on the scene. I was doing
          my duty. You were late.

                    COP 4
          Listen, Wyatt Earp. You just fucked up
          eleven months of hard police work.
          We were about to make the BIGGEST
          BUST OF OUR CAREERS –

                    NICK
          Bullshit. You were late and now you're
          trying to blame me for it. Well, I'm not
          going to take the fall for you assholes!

                    COP 5
          Get him out of here.

                    NICK
          Now, just a minute. I told you the
          registration number of that plane.
          You can find out who owns it –

                    COP 3
          We already know.

                    COP 4
          That plane is registered in San Carlos,
          Honduras. To a U.S. citizen. Samuel
          S. Gundy.

                    NICK
          Well, all you got to do is go talk to him.
          Find out who the pilot was and
          EXTRADITE his ass!

                    COP 3
          Why don't you do it?
          Make a citizen's arrest.

                    NICK
          Maybe I'll just do that.

NICK rises, puts his HELMET underneath his arm.

                    COP 4
          Hey, Cuzco. What's the name of that outfit
          you work for?

                    NICK
          Cactus Security Systems.

COP 4 writes that down.

<u>DOWNTOWN TUCSON</u> EXT DAY

The parking lot of Cactus Security Stystems.

NICK's chief, CAPT. VOGEL, puts an arm around his shoulder.
The other employees are getting in their Company jeeps and cars.
Nobody looks at NICK.

ACROSS THE STREET

COPS 3, 4 and 5 sit in an unmarked car.
They drink coffee and watch.

NICK is trying to explain to his boss about the THREE-WHEELER - sitting
with TIRES SLASHED, MIRRORS BROKEN, SEAT AND HEADLIGHT GONE.

                    NICK
          I don't know how it happened, Captain.

It was cherry when they brought it into
the Police Station –

                    CAPT. VOGEL
          I'm sorry, Nick. It's not just the vehicle.
          It's the overall performance.
          I'm afraid I'm going to have to let you go.

                    NICK
          How about if I resign, Captain Vogel?

                    CAPT. VOGEL
          Sorry, Nick. I look better firing you.
          And this way you can collect Unemployment.
                    (NICK walks away)
          That's the way the world works, Nick.
          But the upside of it is, I get what I need,
          and you get what you deserve.
          Good luck to you!

NICK'S TRAILER   EXT   DAY

A battered Ford station wagon pulls up.

NICK's estranged wife JOLENE gets out. She wears a yellow and white
jumpsuit and has bleached blonde hair.

Her six-year-old daughter JOEY waits in the car as JOLENE walks
towards the –

TRAILER   INT   DAY

NICK is packing his bag.

Half a dozen Hawaiian shirts lie draped across the pull-out bed.
Otherwise, the trailer is completely colorless.

The only decoration is a framed photograph of NICK'S FATHER
- an Arizona State Trooper receiving Trooper of the Year award.

JOLENE appears in the doorway.

                    JOLENE
          So it's true. You're skipping town.

NICK does not reply. Goes on packing his shirts.

                    JOLENE
How long will you be gone?

                    NICK
A few weeks.

                    JOLENE
Then you won't mind if I take the TV.

NICK is preoccupied. He turns on his telephone answering machine.

                    NICK'S VOICE
                (answering machine)
Howdy. This is Nick Cuzco. I'm out on
patrol right now, but if you'd care to
leave a message, uh, do so. And, uh,
don't forget to have a good day!

                    JOLENE
Better change that message, Nick.
Now that you got FIRED and all.

                    NICK
                (trying no to rise to her bait)
Think I should shave my mustache?

                    JOLENE
I don't care if you shave your head.

                    NICK
How's Joey doing?

                    JOLENE
Stop changing the subject, Nick.
You don't care about my kid.

                    NICK
Yes I do, Jolene.

                    JOLENE
No you do not. You can't live with
one person, let alone two. You're
completely selfish and deranged.

                    NICK
Hmm. There's a valuable insight.
So how's DUKE? Keeping FIT?

Staying off the JUICE?

                    JOLENE
He's doing good. We all get along fine.
All three of us.

                    NICK
That's good, Jolene. Be sure and say
HI to DUKE for me!

                    JOLENE
Shut up. He's three times the man
you'll ever be.

She picks up the TV, wraps the cord around it.

                    NICK
How many televisions have you got,
Jolene? You have SIX TVs already.
Do you want my refrigerator?
How about the bed?

                    JOLENE
I don't want your bed.

                    NICK
No! Come on! Have the TRAILER!
Duke can come on by and hitch it up
and you can all go on a wonderful
vacation! ALL THREE OF YOU!

NICK stamps outside.

<u>NICK'S TRAILER</u>   EXT   DAY

NICK carries his bag to his AMC Gremlin.

JOLENE emerges, carrying the TV and OTHER APPLIANCES.

JOEY calls out from the Station Wagon.

                    JOEY
Are you really giving us the trailer,
Nick?

                    NICK
No. You lock up for me, Joey.

Are you still playing ball?

                    JOEY
No. The school caught on fire and
they sent us home.

                    NICK
That's good. Well, keep swinging.
Some day you'll make it to the major
leagues.

                    JOEY
I'm not gonna be a ball player.
I'm gonna be an AQUACULTURIST.

NICK gets in his car and drives away.

TEGUCIGALPA INTERNATIONAL AIRPORT, HONDURAS   EXT   DAY

NICK appears, carrying his bag.

He has shaved off his mustache and dyed his hair BLACK.

He wears sunglasses and a bright Hawaiian shirt.

TAXI DRIVERS accost him.

                    TAXI DRIVERS
          Taxi! Taxi! Mister, taxi!

                    NICK
          San Carlos? San Carlos?

ALL THE TAXI DRIVERS shake their heads and walk away.

NICK approaches a TAXISTA sitting in his cab. He gets in.

                    NICK
          San Carlos.

TAXI   INT   DAY

Crowded, rundown streets. Prostitutes and U.S. army trucks.

NICK's window is missing, and every time the Taxi stops hands shove cashews,
peanuts, lottery tickets and candy skulls in his face.

NICK moves to the other seat.

                    NICK
          Is it far to San Carlos?

                    TAXISTA
          Hotel San Carlos? No. Two dollars.

                    NICK
          Not HOTEL San Carlos. CITY of San
          Carlos. *Ciudad.* Town.

                    TAXISTA
               (frightened)
          Too far! Road no good! Not enough gas!
          We go to Holiday Inn! Better people!
          Better time!

                    NICK
          But I need to go to San Carlos.

                    TAXISTA
          No one goes there! Worst place in Honduras!
          We go to Holiday Inn. Better for you.
          Cheaper taxi fare. My friend!

                    NICK
          I insist we go to San Carlos.

The TAXISTA swings the wheel –

<u>HOLIDAY INN</u> EXT DAY

– and pulls up outside.

The front of the Hotel is sandbagged.

TWO DOORMEN rush out and grab NICK'S BAG.
They run back inside and slam the door.

                    TAXISTA
          Two dollars! Not including TIP.

<u>HOLIDAY INN BAR</u> INT NIGHT

The bar is full of JOURNALISTS, AMERICAN "BUSINESSMEN" with croppe
hair and military bearing, EUROPEAN TOURISTS, and several glamorous and
transient LIBERALS (leaving on the plane next day).

A LOUNGE SINGER croons "Pretty Woman."

NICK enters the bar. He wears khaki pants with map pockets, Nam-style
jungle boots, and a new Hawaiian shirt.

He lays his PITH HELMET down on the bar.

Everyone stares at him.

> NICK
> (to the BARMAN)
Cuba Libre.

> BARMAN
Rum & Coke.

NICK sits down on a stool. He pulls a map from one of his leg pockets.
It is the AAA MAP OF MEXICO AND CENTRAL AMERICA.

A drunken Australian JOURNALIST sits down next to him.

> JOURNALIST
Two whiskey and dry gingers,
quick as you can.

The BARMAN pours two drinks. The JOURNALIST drinks both of them.

> JOURNALIST
> (noticing NICK)
First time in Teegoose?

> NICK
What?

> JOURNALIST
Tegucigalpa. That's what we call it for short.
Easier when filing. I'm getting out, myself.
Not a day too soon. Headed for WestAf.
West Africa. Cover the AIDS. Bloody
nightmare! Tragedy. Terrible tragedy.
Still, serves 'em bloody right, if you
ask me.
> (to BARMAN)
Give me two more!

>   NICK
> Do you know how I can get to San Carlos?
>
>   JOURNALIST
> You don't want to go there, mate.
> Rotten place. Colleague had a foot blown off.
> People go up there, they don't come back.
>
>   NICK
> So how can I get there?
> Can I rent a car?
>
>   JOURNALIST
> Not bloody likely! Bus is the only way.
> And then it's fifty-fifty that you'll hit a
> LANDMINE or be STRAFED!
>
>   NICK
> What time does the bus leave?
>
>   JOURNALIST
> How should I know?
>
>   BARMAN
> Six.
>
>   JOURNALIST
> What line of work you in, Mate? MERC?
>
>   NICK
> I'm an AQUACULTURIST.

COUNTRYSIDE EXT DAY

A decrepit BUS with "Apocalipsis" painted on the side, drives through lush tropical landscape.

NICK shares the roof with TWO OTHER PASSENGERS.

They pass a BURNING CAR.

SOLDIERS watch the car burn. A U.S. MILITARY MAN without insignia confers with a NATIVE OFFICER.

<u>SAN CARLOS</u> EXT DAY

A wretched muddy town with one main street.

The people here stay inside. They are more afraid and paranoid than in
Tucson or Tegucigalpa.

Army tanks are parked and trucks roll through.

NICK is the only passenger to get off the bus.

The bus leaves.

There is a shrine beside the road. NICK takes his PASSPORT, DRIVERS LICENSE,
AIRLINE TICKET and I.D.s and buries them under a rock behind the shrine.

He walks into town.

Beside the PRIVATE HEALTH CLINIC / CASA DE SALUD KRUGER, there is
a general store. NICK enters the store.

<u>GENERAL STORE</u> INT DAY

The store is dark. An OLD MAN and an OLD WOMAN inside.

                    NICK
          Gundy? You know where Señor
          Samuel Gundy lives?

                    OLD WOMAN
          No hay Gundy. No hay gringos here.

NICK walks over to the shelves. Ignoring the fresh fruit and vegetables,
NICK selects a dusty can of SPAM.

<u>SAN CARLOS STREET</u> EXT DAY

A CONVOY consisting of a Land Rover and two jeeps pulls up outside
the General Store. The jeeps are filled with armed BODYGUARDS.

TWO MEN get out of the Land Rover.

One is AMES, a white-haired alcoholic rancher.

The other is THORNTON, last seen beside the DRUG PLANE in the Arizona
desert. THORNTON wears his Yankee cap and carries an M-16.

They make sure the coast is clear, then open the door for the Land Rover's
PASSENGER --

<u>GENERAL STORE</u> INT DAY

NICK is at the counter with his SPAM.

> NICK
> Can opener? To open can?

> OLD MAN
> (shaking head)
> No hay.

ANGLE ON A PAIR OF HIGH HEELS

entering the store. Above them is a sexy summer dress.

CAMILA is the inhabitant of these clothes.

She is the most beautiful woman NICK has ever seen.

THORNTON and AMES follow her into the store.

> CAMILA
> Buenos días, Señora, Señor.
> ¿Llego el paquete de la Ciudad de
> Mexico?

NICK looks at THORNTON, recognises him.
NICK looks quickly away, then back again.

THORNTON looks at NICK. Part of him remembers.

THORNTON takes a step towards him.

> THORNTON
> C'mere, you.

> NICK
> Who, me?

> THORNTON
> Yeah, you. You're in BIG TROUBLE.

> NICK

Oh, yeah?

THORNTON takes another step towards NICK. His M-16 is slung over his shoulder. He reaches for the 9mm PARABELLUM automatic pistol in his belt.

NICK grabs a metal frying pan off the counter.
He whacks THORNTON upside the head.

THORNTON staggers back. He trips and falls, hitting his head against the counter.

AMES rushes to THORNTON, feels for a pulse.

> AMES
> Jesus Christ. He's dead.

NICK picks up THORNTON's pistol. He has eyes only for CAMILA.

> NICK
> I hope I haven't inconvenienced you.

> CAMILA
> You haven't inconvenienced *me*
> at all.

> NICK
> It's always a tragedy when loss of life
> occurs.

> CAMILA
> Indeed.

NICK notices AMES, kneeling beside THORNTON.

> NICK
> You. Help me get him out of here.

NICK spots another ARMED MAN in the doorway.
A local, clad in paramilitary garb. SUICIDA.

> NICK
> You, too! Give a hand with this man.

AMES and SUICIDA look to CAMILA.

> CAMILA
> Do as he says.

AMES and SUICIDA drag THORNTON's body out the door.

NICK crosses to CAMILA.

>   NICK
>   Cigarette?

>   CAMILA
>   I'm already smoking.

CAMILA coldly appraises NICK from head to toe.
AMES shouts to her from the street.

>   AMES
>   Where shall we put the body, MRS GUNDY?

NICK is stunned. CAMILA looks him up and down again.

>   CAMILA
>   In the Land Rover.

>   NICK
>   Duke Palmer. Out of Dallas.

>   CAMILA
>   I'm Camila Gundy. My husband will
>   want to speak with you.

STORE EXT DAY

NICK follows CAMILA out.

AMES and SUICIDA put THORNTON's body in the back seat of the Land Rover.
A small crowd of LOCALS has gathered to watch.

>   CAMILA
>   What line of work are you in, Mr. Palmer?

>   NICK
>   Aquaculture.

>   CAMILA
>   My husband is extremely keen on seafood,
>   so you will enjoy a stimulating talk.

>   NICK

If it's all the same to you, Ma'am, I have
a busy schedule and --

                    CAMILA
You have no choice. If you don't come and
sort this out right now, you will be shot.
Right, Ames?

                    AMES
Like a fuckin' DOG.

                    NICK
In that case... I'd be delighted.

CAMILA jumps in the driver's seat. NICK steps in front of AMES and sits
beside CAMILA.

                    CAMILA
Ames... In the back with Thornton.

MOUNTAINS EXT DAY

The CONVOY travels over rough gravel roads.

Thick pine forests on one side.

Deep chasms on the other.

LAND ROVER INT DAY

NICK and CAMILA in front. THORNTON dead in back, with AMES.

                    NICK
Are you from around here?

                    CAMILA
I'm from Mexico City.

                    NICK
This is a beautiful country. Reminds me
of the Nam.

CAMILA smiles ironically.

                    CAMILA
Viet Nam, huh? Did your daddy take you

there on holiday?

NICK broods, fuming.

                    CAMILA
          I'm sorry. I didn't mean to ruffle your
          feathers.

                    NICK
          That's all right. I wasn't listening.

MOUNTAIN ROAD   EXT   DAY

They turn off onto a dirt road. They pass beneath a STEER'S SKULL
set into a wooden triangle. A sign says,

                    THREE CORNERS RANCH

A couple of heavy-looking LOCALS in army camouflage sit by the gate.
They hold Armalite rifles in their laps.

They doff their baseball caps to MRS CAMILA GUNDY.

LAND ROVER   EXT   DAY

Dust billowing up behind them, they approach SAM GUNDY'S RANCH.

On either side of the road are the overgrown terraces of an untended
coffee plantation. The grounds are thick with parrots and iguanas.

Broken rusting farm vehicles. HUGE DIGGING MACHINES.

Large crates stacked beside a satellite dish.

NO ONE IS WORKING IN THE FIELDS.

LAND ROVER   INT   DAY

CAMILA grabs NICK's pith helmet off his head.
She throws it out the window.

                    CAMILA
          Do yourself a favor.

<u>SAM GUNDY'S RANCH</u>   EXT   AFTERNOON

The main ranch house – known as the Big House – is set atop a small hill
overlooking a vast lake with volcanoes beyond.

The Big House is a modern cantilevered structure in the California 50-'s style.
Made of iron, glass, and synthetic redwood. It looks like a Howard Johnson's
or a Denny's.

A huge-wheeled Toyota 4X4 pickup is parked outside, next to a red Mustang,
a '72 Cadillac Eldorado, and several battered army jeeps.

The OUTBUILDINGS are spread haphazardly in back of the SWIMMING POOL
and TENNIS COURT.

They include Cookhouse, Bunkhouse (a porous shed of brick and tin)
and two Trailers at right angles which serve as offices and KROGER
CASA DE SALUD.

Beyond the OUTHOUSES lies a MILITARY CAMP.

25 or 30 tents, open air showers and latrines, watch tower, training area
and rifle range. Surrounded by a BARBED WIRE FENCE.

The Land Rover parks next to the Toyota 4X4.

AMES, who has been very quiet and servile all thru the ride,
jumps out and runs towards the Big House, shouting.

                         AMES
              He killed Thornton! He killed Thornton!
              Saw it with my own eyes!

COMMOTION.

People come running at the Land Rover from all directions.
SOLDERS, FARM HANDS, AMERICANS in combat gear.

NICK tries to look relaxed and vigilant.
He makes sure to stay close to MRS GUNDY.

A BIG WOODEN DOOR OPENS.

SAM GUNDY COMES OUT.

SAM is a big man. Broad-shouldered, fists like hams.
Pressed white slacks, black cowboy shirt.
Two-toned, handmade cowboy boots.

He has a bullet head, completely bald, and a thick handlebar mustache.

He is followed by his foreman, JOSE GUNTHER, and AMES.

                    AMES
          That's him! He's the one!

                    SAM
          Did you kill Thornton, boy?

                    NICK
          Yes, I did.

                    SAM
          Why on earth did you do that?

NICK is aware of many hostile eyes upon him. He cannot think of an answer.

                    CAMILA
          Thornton started picking on him, Sam.
          Pushing his luck. Acting like an ASSHOLE.
          He got what he deserved.

BRIGGS, a mercenary with a bullwhip coiled in his belt, speaks up angrily.

                    BRIGGS
          That's horseshit, Mrs. Gundy!
          Thornton was here from the beginning.
          He was a DAMN FINE MAN!

                    SAM
          I never liked him. But that ain't the issue.
          The issue is, what I should do with
          THORNTON'S MURDERER.

                    NICK
          Oh man...
                    (eyeing the MANY GUNS aimed at him)
          If you're going to shoot me, shoot me.
          But don't give me this bullshit.
          I hit him with a frying pan.
          You would have done the same.

SAM is impressed.

                    SAM
          What were you doing in San Carlos?

                    NICK
          I came here to get the goods on you, Sam.
          Gather evidence of your unlawful deeds
          and EXTRADITE YOUR ASS.

A long, silent, ominous moment.

All eyes are on SAM. SAM laughs.

                    SAM
          Well, you go right ahead, boy. I've
          nothing to hide. Got a COVER STORY?

                    NICK
          I'm an aquaculturist.

                    SAM
          Ah, shrimps and such. Very good.
          Come on in and join us in the Big House.
          We're about to eat.

<u>BIG HOUSE</u> INT NIGHT

Oversized and opulent, Las Vegas style. Navajo rugs, wagon wheel chandeliers,
thick leather chairs, moose head, Remington and Russell and Georgia O'Keefe
paintings on the walls, blue marlin over the love seat.

The GUNDY CLAN and their MOST TRUSTED FRIENDS are half way
thru dinner.

Seated around the big oak dining table are SAM, CAMILA, LITTLE SAM,
his sister CRYSTAL (both the GUNDY CHILDREN are in their mid twenties.
LITTLE SAM has a bleached blond heavy-metal haircut. CRYSTAL is dressed
in Ralph Lauren western wear). JOSE GUNTHER, JOSHUA SMITH (a
bespectacled Mormon computer expert) and THE KRUGERS – two healthy
middle-aged South African doctors who run the local clinic.

The HOUSEHOLD STAFF bustle in and out with plates of CHINESE FOOD.

NICK sits between GUNTHER and JOSHUA SMITH.

                    SAM
          Things were real bad here 20 years back.
          In Carnicero's day. Diseases, outlaws.
          Alligators. No one's life or property
          was safe.

                    NICK
              (eating compulsively)
          Who's Carnicero?

                    CAMILA
          The Butcher, Duke. He used to be our
          President.

                    AMES
          He was a bad man in many ways --

                    CRYSTAL
          Worse than Hitler.

                    SAM
          Let's not be simplistic. Different places,
          different times, all call for different
          solutions. You can't take a bunch of
          Indians living in the Stone Age and
          give them an Atomic Bomb, the way
          the Government does nowadays.
          Democracy's okay for some, but
          there are HIGHER LAWS.
          You know what I mean, Duke?

                    NICK
          I don't really know the way things
          work around here, Mr. Gundy.
          You seem to have it figured out.

                    SAM
          I wish I did, son. But I don't.
          The only thing I know for sure is,
          nothing stays the same. A man's
          got to be ready.

A PHONE RINGS LOUDLY in another room. A SERVANT enters.

                    SERVANT
          Telephone, Señor Gundy. El Señor Bigelow.

                    SAM
          Excuse me.

SAM GUNDY pulls his napkin from his shirt collar and exits.
MRS KRUGER leans past JOSHUA SMITH, who is staring hungrily at CRYSTAL,
who in turn stares provocatively at NICK.

                    MRS KRUGER
          So. You must be the young man who
          wasted Thornton.

                    NICK
          Not exactly. We were going at it, but I
          can't claim the kill. He hit his head.

                    AMES
               (whispering to LITTLE SAM)
          That's a damn lie. He jumped Thornton.
          Hit him with an iron pan. Briggs says it's
          murder – says we oughta --

                    CRYSTAL
               (gazing at NICK)
          COOL! Wish I'd been there!

NICK studies a framed photograph of SAM with a POLITICIAN and a FLAG.
CAPITOL DOME in the background.

                    NICK
          Does Mr. Gundy have a lot of friends in
          Washington, Miz Gundy?

                    CAMILA
          Sam has friends all over the world,
          on account of his charitable works, Mr...
          I forget your name...

                    NICK
          Palmer. Duke Palmer.

FLASH OF LIGHTNING OUTSIDE.

THUNDER.

                    DR KRUGER
          We get a lot of storms up here, Mr Palmer.
          Many ions in the air. Don't underestimate
          the effects.

SQUEAL OF BRAKES OUTSIDE. OFF SCREEN SHOUTING.

The Big Front Door flies open. COMANDANTE HECTOR CRUZ marches in,
flanked by a group of heavily-armed "CRUZEROS".

HECTOR wears sweat-soaked combat gear. Around his neck are many wooden crosses and gold chains.

HECTOR and his MEN advance on the table like ravenous wolves.

Alarmed, NICK reaches for the gun he took from THORNTON.

MRS KRUGER grabs his hand, restraining him.

                    MRS KRUGER
          Don't excite yourself, dear. They're ours.

HECTOR sits down in SAM's chair and helps himself to Chinese food.

                    CAMILA
          Good evening, Hector. How were your holidays?

                    HECTOR
          They kept me waiting two days in Miami
          Airport. The bastard gringos only guaranteed
          us thirty million. It's bullshit, that's what
          it is. I'm getting out. Democracy is doomed.

SAM GUNDY reappears.

                    SAM
          Nonsense, Hector. Get out of my chair.

SAM pulls HECTOR out of his chair, directs him to another one.

                    SAM
          Your country needs you, Hector, even if
          your wife doesn't. You're a freedom
          fighter, and a patriot. Loved by all.

                    HECTOR
          Are you kidding, Sam? Everybody in this
          pinche country like to put a bullet in my
          back. My precious wife included!
                    (stares intently at each
                    one of them)
          But let me tell you something. If I have
          to die, I'm gonna die LAST.

VERANDAH EXT NIGHT

HECTOR and his CRUZEROS speed away into the night.

HECTOR drives his own Nissan Patrol. He is drunk.

SAM and NICK stand on the verandah, while CAMILA tends to the other
GUESTS within. AMES lurks nearby.

                          AMES
                    (watching HECTOR go)
          He's a fuck-up. But at least he's *our*
          fuck-up.

                          SAM
          I came down here from Iowa in the sixties.
          Me and my dad, Big Sam, in our plane.
          We brought a soil-testing kit and not much
          else. This was all forest then. The soil was
          rich, the water pure. We taught the local
          people how to work. How to fish. How to
          clear land for cattle. It was paradise.

SAM stares at lightning in the distance. Lights a cigar.

                          SAM
          Know anything about *shrimp*, Duke?

                          NICK
          Not really, Mr. Gundy. Big fish are more
          my line.

                          SAM
          Shrimp ranching is the best form of farming
          for a poor nation with cheap labor.
          The people here work for two dollars a day,
          and they're proud to get it.

                          NICK
          Uh... that's great, Mr. Gundy.

                          SAM
          Shrimp farming converts food to edible
          protein eight times more efficiently than
          cattle. It's the opportunity of a lifetime.
          Want to be a part of it?

                          NICK
          I'm not so sure I'd fit in here. You look
          like you're in the middle of a war.

                          SAM

You see those mountains? Beautiful,
aren't they? But you must never be
seduced by beauty, Duke. There are
bandits in those hills. Men who would
rather rape and kill than vote in an
election.
> (he hands NICK a cigar)
Within the confines of this ranch, Duke,
there is peace and equality. And we can
thank Hector and his Freedom Fighters
for that.
> (turns away)
Take your time. Take a few days.
Think about it.

SAM turns immediately back again, holding his temples as if seized by
sudden pain.

> SAM

I'll need your answer in the morning.

Then he is gone. CAMILA appears.

> CAMILA

So, are you going to work here,
Mr Duke Palmer?

> NICK

Do you think I should?

> CAMILA

Yes. I think you should. Why don't you
sleep on it, just to be sure?

> NICK

Where should I sleep on it?

> CAMILA

Where would you like to sleep on it?

> NICK

Well... uh... is there a guest bedroom?

> CAMILA

Sam's GUESTS stay in the Guest Bedroom,
Duke. His MEN stay in the Bunkhouse
with the other MEN. The Bunkhouse is
down that ravine. Good night.

NICK starts down the path towards the ravine.

> CAMILA
> Oh, Mr Palmer!
> (NICK looks back)
> Be careful not to stray into the Garden.
> The dogs are trained to kill after curfew.

MASTER BEDROOM INT NIGHT

A huge bed in the middle of the room. To one side, a desk, a chaise longue,
and the door to the bathroom.

CAMILA slips into her nightgown.

SAM GUNDY sits on the edge of the bed in his underwear, rubbing his temples.

> SAM
> These damn pains are getting worse.
> I might get myself checked out next week.
> Sometimes it sounds like there's an
> airplane landing inside my head.

CAMILA appears not to have heard him. She looks out of the window –

– and sees a TREMENDOUS BOLT OF LIGHTNING shudder across the horizon.

> CAMILA
> I think he's a spy.

> SAM
> Who?

> CAMILA
> Duke Palmer. I'm sure he works for the
> Company. He fits their style: crude,
> obvious, and stupid.

> SAM
> Now, hold on, Camila. There's nothing
> wrong with helping OUR BOYS out now
> and then.

> CAMILA
> Just because they give you money
> doesn't mean they trust you. Let me

                    spend some time with this Duke Palmer.
                    Feel him out. But don't get paranoid.

                              SAM
                    I never get paranoid.

                              CAMILA
                    Yeah, sure.

                              SAM
                    I don't have time to get paranoid,
                    Camila. There are other matters...
                    more important...

He goes to his desk and sits down, starts shuffling papers around.

                              SAM
                    Are you with me, Camila?

                              CAMILA
                    You know I am, Sam. All the way to
                    she end.

She crosses the room, puts her arm around him. Kisses him.

                              CAMILA
                    Oh, Sam. Can't we take off for a few
                    months? Just the two of us.
                    Let's go to Paris.

                              SAM
                    You know, Camila, nothing would make
                    me happier than to see you satisfied.
                    But I can't leave the Ranch right now.
                    Too many things are happening.
                    Maybe after the rains –

SUDDENLY there is a JOLT OF LIGHTNING outside the window.
They both stare at it, transfixed. The LIGHTNING enters the room,
circles SAM's head, and enters him.

SAM falls to the floor, jerking and flapping his arms and legs.

CAMILA kneels beside him, terrified.

                              CAMILA
                    Are you all right?

SAM looks up at her, a beatific smile on his face.

                    SAM
          NEVER BETTER!

He reaches up and pulls her to him. She straddles him.

                    SAM
          CAN YOU FEEL IT?

Another CRACK OF LIGHTNING, as SAM jerks himself into CAMILA.

RANCH   EXT   MORNING

NICK follows an irrigation ditch through an abandoned coffee terrace.
He is alone.

He comes upon a large tin shed. Looks inside.
The shed is piled high with wooden crates, marked –

          SHRIMPS – KEEP REFRIGERATED

NICK hears the sound of rifle fire.

RIFLE RANGE   EXT   MORNING

NICK pauses to watch an ill-equipped platoon of SOLDIERS firing at wooden
targets. Directing them are BRIGGS and JOSHUA SMITH.

                    SMITH
               (yelling)
          You mopes couldn't shoot your way
          out of a paper bag! Reload! *¡Rapido!*

                    NICK
          Bad ordnance you got there.

                    BRIGGS
          What do you know about it?

                    NICK
          Not much. I'm a multiple conversion
          man, myself. Give me a Springfield
          Armory Omega and turn me loose.
          Interchangeable barrels. That
          universal slide assembly with the

lug in the recoil spring. That's action.

                    BRIGGS
          You're a regular COMMANDO, aintcha?
          Listen here, Johnny-on-the-Spot.
          Thornton was a personal friend of mine.
          He saved my life. In NAM.

                    NICK
          Know what I've noticed about guys
          that went to NAM? The real men never
          say a thing about it. The ones that talk
          about it all the time are either PSYCHOS
          or LIARS.

All is quiet on the RIFLE RANGE. BRIGGS reaches for a weapon –

CAMILA GUNDY appears.

                    CAMILA
          Making friends, Duke? I need you to
          drive me some place. Everyone else
          seems to be too busy.

                    NICK
          At your service, Miz Gundy.
          CARRY ON, YOU MEN!

He follows her towards the Big House.
BRIGGS foams at the mouth, staring after NICK.

LAKESIDE DOCK EXT DAY

CAMILA leads NICK down to the lake, where a Cris Craft is tied up to a
simple dock.

The lake is big, with mountains and volcanes on the far side.

                    CAMILA
          I thought we'd take the boat. It's
          so boring in the Land Rover.
          And last night they blew up the bridge.

                    NICK
          Who did?

                    CAMILA

                    The rebels, I expect. Nothing serious.
                    Just a calling card.

They step down into the Cris Craft, CAMILA behind the wheel.

The 50 h.p. Johnson motor gives a stuttering roar.
She guides the boat into the middle of the lake.

LAKE EXT DAY

They zip along, a plume of water on both sides of the speed boat.
NICK settles back, happy to be alive and alone with CAMILA.

ISLAND EXT DAY

CAMILA guides the Cris Craft towards a small island.

ISLAND EXT DAY

NICK follows CAMILA up a rocky path. No one is around.
The silence is strange and ominous.

They approach the ruins of an ancient town. NICK follows CAMILA into
an overgrown garden. The thick green foliage is sensual and protective.

They are both hot and sweaty. CAMILA spreads out a towel from her
beach bag and sits down. Lying back, she looks invitingly at NICK.

                    CAMILA
          So, Duke Palmer. What do you have
          to say for yourself?

NICK considers his situation. He likes what he thinks he finds.

                    NICK
          I think I might be one of the luckiest
          guys in the world right now.

                    CAMILA
          Why do you say that?

NICK takes off his shirt. He is very confident, very cool.
CAMILA rubs his foot, encouraging him.

NICK sets his 9mm PARABELLUM on the ground. As he starts to remove

his pants, CAMILA pulls a .38 REVOLVER from her beach bag and aims
it straight at NICK.

                              CAMILA
                    Who sent you here?

NICK looks at her, uncomprehending.

                              CAMILA
                    Who told you to kill my husband?

                              NICK
                    Nobody.

                              CAMILA
                    You're working for the C.I.A.

                              NICK
                    No, I'm not. I don't work for anyone.
                    I'm strictly freelance. I'm just down
                    here looking for work, like everybody
                    else.

                              CAMILA
                    Don't lie, Duke.

                              NICK
                    I'm not lying. My luck ran out in the US.
                    I was a Texas Ranger. But I got busted.

                              CAMILA
                    What did you get busted for?

                              NICK
                    Messing with the Captain's wife.

CAMILA pulls the trigger. NICK shuts his eyes. CLICK.
An empty cylinder. She puts the gun away. NICK opens his eyes.

                              CAMILA
                    I'm still not sure I believe you.

In the distance, MORTAR FIRE is heard. CAMILA stands.

                              NICK
                    The Ranch?

                              CAMILA

The rebels. Every day, they get a
little closer.

CAMILA walks back towards the boat.
NICK struggles into his pants and follows.

<u>LAKESIDE DOCK</u> EXT DAY

The boat pulls up to the dock.

LITTLE SAM, CRYSTAL and the KRUGERS are splashing about.
They drink bloody marys and eat chips and hot dogs.

NICK and CAMILA climb onto the dock.

> CRYSTAL
>> Having fun?

> NICK
>> Always.

The MORTAR FIRE continues in the distance.

> DR KRUGER
>> We should think about inoculating you,
>> Palmer.

> NICK
>> I got my shots.

> MRS KRUGER
>> You'd be surprised how many VICIOUS
>> and MALIGNANT PARASITES there
>> are in the jungle here. You're not in
>> California now, Herr Palmer.

> NICK
>> Never was.

He starts after CAMILA, heading for the Big House.
CRYSTAL pops out of the water, breathless in her bikini.

> CRYSTAL
>> Did you have a nice RIDE?

> NICK
>> Nice enough. Your mom's a terrific

guide.

                    CRYSTAL
          She's not my mother. My mother is
          in Iowa. How *old* do you think I *am,*
          anyhow?

Before NICK can reply, JOSHUA SMITH roars up in a jeep.

                    SMITH
          Where the hell have you been, Palmer?
          You're not getting paid just to hang out.

                    NICK
          I was following orders.

                    SMITH
          Your orders are to come with me.
                    (before NICK can argue)
          To the AIRSTRIP.

Interested, NICK gets in the jeep.

AIRSTRIP EXT DAY

A desolate field on a far corner of the Ranch. Out of sight of the Big House
and Outbuildings.

Rusting fuel tanks and a couple of decrepit Cessnas.

A TWIN-ENGINED TRANSPORT is being loaded up.
It is *not* the same plane as NICK saw in the Arizona desert,
though it bears the logo, LONGHORN AIR TRANSPORT.

SMITH pulls up. He and NICK get out.

SOLDIERS load the plane with large CRATES and smaller BOXES.
The BOXES are stenciled, SHRIMP – KEEP REFRIGERATED.

BRIGGS and a couple of SOLDIERS struggle to get a heavy crate aboard
the plane. BRIGGS shouts at NICK.

                    BRIGGS
          Come on, Palmer. Give us a hand!

SMITH shoves a clipboard and a pen in NICK's face.

                    SMITH
               Sign here.

                     NICK
                  (signing)
               What is it?

                    SMITH
               Your release, in case you get killed.

                    BRIGGS
               PALMER!

NICK climbs into the hatchway, helps them manhandle the crate on board.

                     NICK
               What's in this?

                    BRIGGS
               Christmas presents.

PLANE INT DAY

AMES is in the pilot seat, checking the controls and flicking switches.
He indicates a SEAT BELT attached to the wall.

                     AMES
               Put that on.

NICK doesn't move. BRIGGS climbs aboard, checks the PARACHUTES
attached to the LARGEST CRATES.

The SOLDIERS help BRIGGS slam the door.

                     NICK
               Hold on, Briggs. I'm not going on any
               airplane ride.

The PLANE is already taxiing.

                    BRIGGS
               Orders of Mr Gundy.

PLANE EXT SUNSET

In flight. Dense green jungle beneath.

Lakes and volcanoes. Huge rivers curve.

<u>BIG HOUSE LIBRARY</u> INT NIGHT

The lights are low. SAM GUNDY sits in a big leather chair.
MRS KRUGER stands behind him. She holds her hands over his head.
FEELING HIS AURA.

        MRS KRUGER
    Your aura is completely altered.
    It is green and yellow now. I have never
    known an aura like it. It has entirely
    changed.

FLICKER. She jumps back, as if suffering a mild electric shock.

        MRS KRUGER
    You are a vessel for great power, Sam.
      (she grabs his hand)
    But your palm contradicts this.
    According to your lines, you have no
    chance of success. You cannot survive,
    alone.

        SAM
    I am not alone. I have Camila.
    And the Ranch.

        MRS KRUGER
    You are in great danger, Sam.
    You need help and assistance.
    You cannot trust your friends.

The thump of an AMPLIFIED BASS and ELECTIC GUITAR crash thru the room.
"SATISFACTION."

MRS KRUGER shakes her head.

        MRS KRUGER
    I've lost it. The vibrations are gone.

<u>BIG HOUSE</u> EXT NIGHT

Thru the big windows we see SAM GUNDY and MRS KRUGER in the dark
library. In the Big Room adjacent, CRYSTAL, LITTLE SAM and several

sleazy PLAYBOYS and HOOKERS from Tegucigalpa are having a
rock & roll party.

CRYSTAL and LITTLE SAM whale away on electric guitars.

<u>PLANE</u> INT NIGHT

Still airborne. BRIGGS yells at NICK, above the engine noise.
He points at the CRATES, mimes opening the door.

                    BRIGGS
               (shouting)
          I open the door! You kick this box out!
          Then you kick this box out!

                    NICK
               (shouting, pointing at
                the smaller boxes)
          What about the SHRIMP BOXES?
          When do I push THEM out?

                    BRIGGS
          Don't! Push! The Shrimp Boxes!

                    NICK
          You want me to push the Shrimp Boxes!

                    BRIGGS
          Whatever! You! Do! Don't! Push!
          The SHRIMP BOXES! If you do, you're
          going after them!

                    NICK
          Anything you say, ASSHOLE!

<u>PLANE</u> EXT NIGHT

BRIGGS and NICK stand in the hatchway kicking out the CRATES.
The CRATES' PARACHUTES open and they float gently down.

BRIGGS and NICK have no parachutes.

Flashes of GUNFIRE below.

<u>PLANE</u> INT NIGHT

All that remains of the cargo is 25 or 30 boxes.

AMES has produced a bottle of brandy. Still at the controls, he reads a newspaper. NICK and BRIGGS drink beer from a cooler.

NICK eyes the SHRIMP BOXES.

AMES folds the paper up and thrusts it at BRIGGS.

                AMES
        Ha! Told you so!

BRIGGS stares at the headline of the Miami Herald.
He grunts, and throws the paper on the deck. NICK picks it up.

ANGLE ON THE HEADLINE

          RESISTANCE LEADER TIED TO CIA
         DENIES INVOLVEMENT IN MASSACRE

Above a photograph of HECTOR CRUZ.

              BRIGGS
        Hector's never gonna win this war.
        Know why? I'll tell you why. He's a
        FUCKING PLAYBOY FUCK-UP!
        That's why the FUCKING COMPANY
        is gonna FUCKING CUT HIM LOOSE.
        When the shit comes down –

He runs a finger across his throat.

                AMES
        The shit's never gonna come down, Briggs.
        You talk like you believe that ideology crap.
        This is a range war. Ranchers versus
        homesteaders. No side ever wins.

              BRIGGS
        I'm sick of your kind, Ames. Know why?
        Because you won't admit what's wrong
        with this country is it's run by FUCKING
        PLAYBOYS! If it was up to me, I'd shoot
        the lot of 'em –
            (to NICK)
        – starting with YOU, Palmer!

                    NICK
          Whatever you say, Briggs.

                    BRIGGS
          If you're expecting to make it on this
          Ranch, you better realize YOUR PLACE.
          You're BUNKHOUSE, Palmer. Not BIG
          HOUSE. You're a WORKING SCUM,
          like me and Ames!

                    AMES
          Speak for yourself, Briggo. I got my own
          ranch. I got six men working for me --

                    NICK
          You got a job for me, Ames?

                    BRIGGS
          Shut up, Palmer.

                    AMES
          Seriously, Duke. You better stop trying
          to POOCH the boss's old lady. Many have
          tried. Many have died. I never slept with
          any woman but my wife, in my whole
          life. In my day --

Thru the cockpit window, all three see a FLYING SAUCER.

Glowing brightly, it parallels their flight path for ten seconds,
then hurtles away.

They look at each other in stunned silence.

                    NICK
          Did you see that?

                    AMES
          Sometimes you see things when you're
          up here... 'specially when you're alone...

                    BRIGGS
          No, you don't. Stress. Fatigue.
          Tricks of the mind.

The RADIO SQUAWKS. They all jump with fright.

                    RADIO VOICE

                    Request discrete transponder code
                    for traffic separation –

                              BRIGGS
                         (into radio)
                    This is seven eighty eight. We're a non-
                    scheduled military flight approaching
                    Holmstead. Requesting landing
                    permission –

AIRFIELD EXT NIGHT

The plane lands on a tarmac runway.

A little blue truck pulls in front of them. On the back, a sign reads,

                         FOLLOW ME

                    WELCOME TO HOLMSTEAD
                       AIR FORCE BASE

PLANE INT NIGHT

NICK peers thru the window.

                              NICK
                    Wait a minute! If you guys think
                    you're gonna set me up –
                         (pulls out his gun)
                    Turn this plane around!

                              AMES
                    Calm down, Palmer. We ain't gonna
                    be here long.

They taxi towards a HANGAR. NICK sees the CONTROL TOWER –
it too says, HOLMSTEAD FLORIDA.

The plane rolls to a halt. BRIGGS opens the hatch.
NICK's hand hovers near his gun.

AIRFIELD EXT NIGHT

The hangar doors are closed. U.S. AIR FORCE PERSONNEL run from a
side door to the PLANE. ARC LIGHTS.

The AIRMEN unload the boxes and fuel the plane.

                    BRIGGS
          Jump out, Palmer. Run away.
          You'll make it.

A SMILING CORPORAL brings them coffee in plastic 7-11 cups.

The SHRIMP BOXES are loaded onto an electric baggage cart.
The cart is driven quickly away.

Two more carts arrive. LARGE WOODEN CRATES are piled aboard the plane.

                    CORPORAL
          See you next week!

PLANE INT NIGHT

BRIGGS slams the door shut. The plane taxis away.

The plane is so full of CRATES that there is barely room left.
NICK hasn't moved.

                    BRIGGS
          Can't take it, huh?

AIRFIELD EXT NIGHT

The plane barely makes it off the runway.

ABOVE HONDURAS EXT DAWN

The aircraft is tiny against a magnificent sky.

Jungle and ocean below.

SAM GUNDY'S AIRSTRIP EXT MORNING

The plane lands. A jeep waits for them.

BIG HOUSE EXT MORNING

The jeep drops AMES and BRIGGS at the Bunkhouse.

NICK marches up the ravine, passes a Mercedes limousine and several armored-looking cars.

He is determined and pissed-off.

BIG HOUSE INT MORNING

NICK barges in. GUNTHER and other STAFF try to restrain him, but he brushes them aside.

                         NICK
              Out of my way!

NICK opens the Big Door to the –

BIG ROOM INT MORNING

SAM GUNDY is with an American, WORTH BIGELOW III.
BIGELOW is tall, patrician, confident. The man in the framed picture.

They hover over a briefcase filled with HUNDRED DOLLAR BILLS.
JOSHUA SMITH is feeding the bills into a COUNTING MACHINE.

                         NICK
              Mr Gundy, I need to speak to you. Alone.

                         SAM
              Duke, I'd like you to meet Worth Bigelow.
              From Washington. You and I both work
              for Mr Bigelow. Don't we, Worth?

                         BIGELOW
              Well... I wouldn't put it quite that way, Sam.
                   (extends a hand)
              Worth Bigelow.

NICK idly shakes hands, glares at SAM GUNDY.

                         NICK
              Last night I flew on your plane to Miami,
              Florida. We unloaded drugs. We also
              carried crates of weapons. We had no
              parachutes, no break, and the pilot
              was drunk. I got shot at and worked

sixteen hours straight.

SAM
What do you mean, "Drugs"
Duke? You ferried seafood last
night. To Guatemala City.
Why, I'm not sure I even have
a plane that could make it all
the way to Miami on one tank
o'gas. As for those crates, Duke,
they were tractor parts.
Things are a lot slower than
you think down here.

BIGELOW
Pleased to meet you, Duke.
Pleased and proud. Very proud
of your work here. There's a
lot of people up in DC that are
proud of you. Damned proud.
A lot of eyes are on you.
Everyone up there loves Sam
Gundy. There is no better man
to learn from, no keener patriot,
Nor better American.

NICK
Well...

BIGELOW
How about a piece of lobster, Duke?
Some caviar?

NICK grabs a spoon and wolfs down caviar.

NICK
Thanks, Mister Err...

BIGELOW
My friends call me Worth. Champagne?

NICK
I'll have some for later.
(takes a bottle)
I guess I'll just keep on doing my best here
at the Ranch. Sorry to come barging in
like this, Mr Gundy. Mr Worth...

BIGELOW offers NICK a book on bees.

BIGELOW
Something to read?

NICK
No, thanks. I'm all dirty, sir. I think I'll
head back to the Bunkhouse and HOSE
OFF.

SAM
Use the bathroom upstairs, Duke. Hot water.

Beats the Bunkhouse, any day,

                    NICK
          Thanks, Mr Gundy.
               (backing out)
          Gennelmen...

NICK exits.

                    BIGELOW
          Are you sure he's okay?

                    SAM
          No problem.

                    BIGELOW
          I'll run a check on him anyway.

RANCH EXT DAY

BRIGGS hoses himself down behind the Bunkhouse.
AMES waits to be next, shivering, holding his bar of soap and little towel.

The BIG HOUSE, on a hill behind them, dominates the scene.

BATHROOM INT DAY

NICK enters the Master Bathroom of the Big House.

The room is full of steam and mirrors, towels all over the floor,
body lotions, shampoos everywhere. Roman in style.

NICK pops the Champagne cork and takes a long drink from the bottle.

He strips off his filthy clothes and opens the door to the BIG SHOWER.
Steam billows out. Streams of hot water cascade over MRS CAMILA GUNDY.

NICK covers his eyes in horror at his indiscretion.

                    CAMILA
          What are you doing here?

                    NICK
          Your husband... sent me... hot water...

She stares down at his enormous boner.

                    CAMILA
          Ah. Well, now that you're here you might
          as well come in.

LIBRARY   INT   DAY

GUNDY, SMITH, and BIGELOW stare at financial figures on SMITH's computer.

                    SAM
          Don't get me wrong. I love Hector like
          a brother. And he's been a big asset.
          But lately, he's not banging on all eight...

                    BIGELOW
          Sam, we see eye to eye as always.
          And State feels the same as we do.
          It's a hard decision, but STEELHAMMER
          wants you to pull the plug on him.

                    SAM
          Pull the plug..?

                    BIGELOW
          Eliminate him.

SAM frowns, distressed at his old friend's fate.
The sound of running water fills his ears.
STATIC ripples and flows across the screen.

SHOWER INT DAY

RICK and CAMILA in the throes of passion.
Hot water streaming over them.

BIG ROOM INT DAY

SAM stares into the static of the computer monitor.

Big veins stand out on his forehead.

BANG! A POWER SURGE shorts out the computer.

JOSHUA SMITH is thrown across the room.

BIG HOUSE INT LATER

NICK comes down the stairs, whistling. He is very clean.

He passes SAM GUNDY, emerging from the library.

                    SAM
          Feel better, Duke?

                    NICK
          I feel great, Mr Gundy!

BUNKHOUSE INT DAY

NICK wakes up on his bunk. The late afternoon sun pours through the
Bunkhouse. An OLD MAN sweeps the floor.

                    NICK
          Buenos días, Señor.
          What time is it?

                    OLD MAN
              (in Spanish, subtitled)
          Too late for time.

                    NICK
          Where are the others?

                    OLD MAN
              (in Spanish, subtitled)
          I was in your country once. Lancaster,
          Pennsylvania. I could hold my breath
          under water ten minutes. You people
          are all crazy. HA HA HA! What are you
          doing here? You don't even know.
          You don't even know what I am saying.
          HA HA HA! You will die. That is for sure.

                    NICK
          Gracias! Amigo!

NICK gets up and goes outside.

RANCH EXT DAY

A PHOTO SESSION is in progress in the MILITARY CAMP.

TWO VIDEO CREWS and various PRESS PHOTOGRAPHERS record events
staged by GUNDY and the KRUGERS.

A VACCINATION CENTER has been set up. SOLDIERS in fresh clean uniforms,
led by SUICIDA in a white coat, stick needles in SMALL CHILDREN's arms.

CRYSTAL is dressed in a Red Cross Nurse's uniform, holding babies.
CAMILA hands out Tylenol and condoms.

                         BIGELOW
               These people want Democracy so badly
               they can taste it!

The VIDEO CAMERA pans over to a LADY JOURNALIST with microphone.

                      LADY JOURNALIST
               Last night I saw campesinos who can
               barely read poring over books on
               Political Science and American History,
               painfully teaching themselves those
               things they need to know to keep their
               country free --

BIGELOW nods and puts his arms round two freshly-scrubbed SOLDIERS.

GUNDY, AMES and BRIGGS stand off to the side, watching the MEDIA CIRCUS.
NICK joins them.

It is JOSHUA SMITH's turn to be interviewed.

                         SMITH
               Ezekiel says that fire and brimstone will
               be rained upon the enemies of God's
               People. That means they'll be destroyed
               by Nuclear Weapons. Ezekiel tells us that
               Gog, the Nation that will lead all the Powers
               of Darkness against Israel ==

                         BRIGGS
               Somebody shut him up.

                         AMES
               The man's a wacko. I say we run him
               off the Ranch.

                         SAM

Quit bellyachin'. Smith's young. Still full
of piss and vinegar. You should have seen
me when I was his age. Regular hellraiser.

                    BRIGGS
Yeah, Sam. But this is national TV.

The VIDEO CREWS get tired of SMITH and ZOOM IN on SAM GUNDY.

                    BLACK JOURNALIST
Mr Gundy! You're a local rancher here
and say publicly you're NON POLITICAL.
Yet the Democratic Resistance has a military
base here on your Ranch. Do you see this
as a contradiction?

                    LADY JOURNALIST
People say you work for the C.I.A. Mr Gundy.
That you run drugs off this Ranch.

                    SAM
Well, Jane. I guess there are some people
who'll say just about anything to blacken
a man's name. I'm just a simple rancher.
I'm not smart enough to do these complicated
things. But I will say this. Here at Three
Corners Ranch, we won't deny help to a
wounded man, no matter what side he's on.

SAM grabs NICK, and pushes him in front of the CAMERAS.

                    SAM
Here's a young man that just started work
with us. A young scientist, Dr Salvatore.
Duke Salvatore. Tell 'em about our plans
to end hunger in this country, Duke.

                    NICK
                 (terrified)
What? What plans?

                    SAM
Shrimp farm.

SAM walks away. NICK blinks at the cameras.

                    NICK
Well, we're gonna get these shrimp...

Put 'em in ponds... and farm 'em...

The REPORTERS lose interest in NICK. BRIGGS steps forward.

> BRIGGS
> I want to say something about my
> experience with the Red Cross. You talk
> about the C.I.A., but in my opinion the
> Red Cross are completely corrupt.
> They are staffed with degenerates.
> They hoard money and do nothing for
> the sick and wounded. During the
> Battle of Hue, I saw my friends dying
> from lack of medical attention, and
> the Red Cross is standing there handing
> out STALE DONUTS and COFFEE.
> Another time –

The JOURNALISTS turn off their CAMERAS and walk away.

BIG HOUSE   EXT   DAY

BIGELOW and his ENTOURAGE prepare to depart.
SAM and CAMILA walk him to his Mercedes.

> CAMILA
> Nice to see you again, Wort. But are you
> sure you cannot stay till morning?
> The roads are treacherous at night.

> BIGELOW
> I must fly back early tomorrow. My wife
> will kill me if I stay another day. We're
> buying my daughter a pony. You know
> how kids are.

> SAM
> TV session go okay for you today, Worth?
> Photo session?

> BIGELOW
> Yes, Sam, it was satisfactory. It could have
> been better. A little less spontaneous.

> SAM
> Yeah. Well, anyway. What can you do.
> About that O.P.I.C loan you said might be

possible, I still haven't heard from D.C.

                    BIGELOW
Sam, these things take time. Once
Hector's out of the way, the log jam
will loosen up.

                    SAM
Sure, Worth, Buddy. But I got a Ranch
to run –

                    BIGELOW
And you're doing a good job. But you're
no longer a TOP TEN PRIORITY.
However, you are still in the SECOND
TEN.

BIGELOW gets into his Mercedes. The door clicks shut.

BIGELOW and his BODYGUARDS lead the convoy of "TV" Toyotas down the
road into the jungle.

BIG HOUSE   INT   DUSK

SAM GUNDY stamps into the Big Room, enraged. CAMILA follows.

                    SAM
That ARROGANT ASSHOLE! He has the
nerve to come down here for two days,
tell me how to run my operation,
keep money that's mine, bureaucrat
me to death, LIE TO ME –

                    CAMILA
You did a good job, Sam. You'll look
handsome on TV.

SAM grabs a SHOTGUN from the RIFLE RACK and loads it.

                    SAM
I've been here 25 years. I've had
experiences in these mountains that
he doesn't even know exist! Little
shit! He said I'm in the SECOND TEN!
What does THAT MEAN?

                    CAMILA

                    It means you're about as important
                    to him as Nigeria.

                              SAM
          SHIT!

CAMILA goes upstairs. SAM aims his RIFLE at the TV.

The TV EXPLODES before SAM can fire.

BEACH EXT DUSK

AFTER SUNSET.

All the ANIMALS in the hills begin to howl.

BUNKHOUSE EXT NIGHT

JOSE GUNTHER sits outside the Bunkhouse playing his guitar.
He strums the melancholy ballad, "Niño Perdido."

He stares at CAMILA GUNDY, silhouetted in her window.

BUNKHOUSE INT NIGHT

NICK makes a selection from his set of Hawaiian shirts.
TWO OTHER MERCENARIES sit on the bunks opposite.
They clean their rifles and watch an ACTION ADVENTURE VIDEO.

                         MERC 1
          I'm taking four M-16 grenades, my FAL,
          500 rounds of 7.62 NATO ball, ten full
          banana clips, three cans of tuna,
          three cans of condensed milk,
          two canteens, and an M72 LAW.
          That should cover it.

                         MERC 2
          You're travelling too light, mate.
          I'm packing double that ordnance,
          and I ain't carrying no food.

He looks around.

                         MERC 2

                    I'll be glad to see the back of this
                    shithole. And everybody in it.

                              MERC 1
                         (glaring at NICK)
                    Reckon we should KILL A COP before
                    we go. Hey, son. Ready to die for your
                    beliefs?

                              NICK
                    I have no beliefs. Don't need 'em.
                         (chooses a shirt)
                    Where are you guys going?

                              MERC 2
                    We're headed for the border. Then
                    Panama City. Sell all our gear and
                    buy a sailboat. Sail up the coast.

                              MERC 1
                    You ever been in a sailboat? It's
                    fantastic. The silence and the
                    luminosity. It's the closest you can
                    get to God.

                              NICK
                         (standing up)
                    Give my best to God.

BUNKHOUSE EXT NIGHT

NICK emerges and stands next to JOSE GUNTHER.

GUNTHER has been joined by OTHER MUSICIANS.
All are serenading MRS GUNDY in her window.

NICK watches, then strolls up the ravine towards the HOUSE.

The SONG continues.

BIG HOUSE EXT NIGHT

NICK creeps closer to the Big House.

The jeeps and trucks of HECTOR CRUZ are parked outside.

NICK pauses beneath the verandah.

He sees SMITH with his face pressed to the window, looking in.

NICK comes up behind him.

SMITH is spying on SAM GUNDY and HECTOR CRUZ.

> NICK
> What are you doing, Smith?

> SMITH
> Cruz is in there. Bugging Mr Gundy.
> Wasting Mr Gundy's time.
> They're gonna waste him.

ANGLE THRU THE WINDOW –

on SAM and HECTOR CRUZ, smoking cigars and drinking brandy in the Library.

> NICK
> Waste who?

> SMITH
> Hector Cruz. He's all washed up.
> He's supposed to be in charge of the
> Democratic Resistance but he spends
> all his time at the track in Miami.
> He's the reason we're not doing our
> job here. Morale is at an all-time low.

He spits at the window.

LIBRARY INT NIGHT

HECTOR is subdued and weary. SAM wears his dressing gown. LOG FIRE.

> HECTOR
> Sam. People I trust tell me you are
> involved in a plot to kill me. A Company
> plot. As an old friend, tell me if this
> is true.

> SAM
> Absolutely not, Hector.
> Who told you about this plan?

                    HECTOR
          As you know, Sam, I am not a man who
          fears death. When my time comes,
          I'll meet it like a man.

                    SAM
          I know that about you, Hector.

                    HECTOR
          Because I could go back to Miami
          tomorrow. My bags could be packed
          in three hours. I have a girlfriend there.
          A couple houses. It would be fine –

                    SAM
          Hector, there's no reason why the C.I.A.
          would want to kill you. The commies
          would rejoice at that. We may have our
          occasional differences, but you're
          the Point Man, Hector.
          This is your country, and it's all
          being done for you.

                    HECTOR
          Thanks, Sam. But let me know if you
          hear anything, okay?

                    SAM
          I certainly will, Hector. You have my
          word on that.

The door opens. CRYSTAL and some sleazy SONS OF LOCAL BIGWIGS
stumble in. They are drunk and carry bottles of Champagne.

                    CRYSTAL
          Oh, hi, dad. Hi, Hector. You guys
          still plotting to destroy the world?

BIG HOUSE EXT NIGHT

JOSHUA SMITH presses his face and body against the window in an agony
of paranoia and desire for CRYSTAL.

                    SMITH
          Somebody's got to TAKE CHARGE
          HERE! TAKE ACTION! GNNNN!
          Things are OUT OF CONTROL!

<u>CAMILA'S BEDROOM</u> INT NIGHT

CAMILA looks down at the sports cars and army jeeps that clog the drive.
The iron girders of the house vibrate with DISCO MUSIC.

She sees NICK, walking down the driveway.

<u>DIRT ROAD</u> EXT NIGHT

NICK walks away from the Ranch.

DISCO MUSIC hammers in the distance.

He walks till it gets quieter.

SUICIDA and a well-scrubbed SOLDIER pass him, leading two prisoners.
The PRISONERS have razor wire tied around their necks.

HEADLIGHTS swing up behind NICK.

CAMILA GUNDY pulls up in the Land Rover.

                    CAMILA
          Going somewhere?

                    NICK
          Just taking a walk.

                    CAMILA
          Get in.

<u>LAND ROVER</u> INT NIGHT

CAMILA drives extremely fast. NICK is unsure of her mood.

In silence, they hurtle up the hill.

<u>MESA</u> EXT NIGHT

The Land Rover speeds across a flat-topped mesa.
It parks near the edge. MOON OVERHEAD.

NICK and CAMILA climb out.

MILLIONS OF STARS above them.   LIGHTNING DISPLAY below.

                    NICK
          Sure is a lot of lightning.

                    CAMILA
          That's the Ranch down there. My husband
          owns that valley, and the mountains,
          and the mountains beyond.

                    NICK
          Does he own everything?

                    CAMILA
          Everything as far as the border.

NICK embraces her. They kiss. CAMILA breaks away.

                    CAMILA
          I heard somewhere about this legend.
          It concerns the Ranch, or rather the land
          that the Ranch is on. The *Conquistadores*
          camped there when they first came from
          Spain. They did terrible things to the
          Indians. Enslaved them. Finally the
          Gods got angry and put a curse on them.
          The Spanish were turned into animals
          and devoured themselves.

                    NICK
          Why did you come here?

                    CAMILA
          I fell in love with Sam. It was a
          terrible thing. Broke up his marriage.
          His wife was really fucked up about it.
          She set Sam's kids against me.
          Everyone always loses in a triangle.

                    NICK
          I'm mad for you. I've been thinking
          of nothing else since I first saw you.
          The men were serenading you tonight.
          And I felt like a fucking god because
          we had made love.

                    CAMILA
          We must never see each other again.

                    NICK
          What? Tell me I've got to work
          forever at the Ranch, but don't
          tell me we an never see each other –

                    CAMILA
          We must never see each other.
          We must never do this –
                    (she kisses him)
          Or this –
                    (she gropes him)
          Or this –
                    (she crushes his body
                      against hers)
          Again.

CAMILA walks towards the Land Rover.
NICK is too stunned and confused to move.

                    NICK
          You're wrong.

                    CAMILA
          No. It is too dangerous. If we
          continue, we may destroy
          ourselves and everybody else.

She gets in, and drives off. Leaving him alone on the edge of the mesa.

THUNDER. A dark cloud covers the Moon. It starts to rain.

NICK howls like a wounded animal.

ROAD THRU THE JUNGLE EXT DAWN

The dirt road has turned to liquid mud.
The trees drip from the recent rainfall.

NICK plods along, bound for the Ranch.

The sun is only just up, and it is already scorching.

Insects buzz around his head.

NICK hears the sound of a SMALL PLANE.

<u>AIRSTRIP</u> EXT MORNING

NICK pushes through the foliage.

A the far end of the airfield, he sees a TWIN-ENGINED PLANE –
the same plane that THORNTON landed in the Arizona desert.

The KRUGERS herd TEN CHILDREN aboard the aircraft.
The CHILDREN wear party hats and carry balloons.
One of them carries a small KITTEN.

YOUNG SAM plays with the CHILDREN as they board the plane.
He wears a red curly wig and a false nose.

NICK stares at the idyllic scene.

He is terrified, as if he has seen the DEVIL.

<u>DOCK</u> EXT MORNING

SAM and CAMILA GUNDY supervise the loading of a motorized DUGOUT CANOE.
They are a handsome couple, athletic and attractively dressed.

GUNTHER and THREE LOCALS are trying to drag a HIDEOUS DEAD ANIMAL
from the lake with hooks. The creature has bulging eyes and a thick snout.

NICK trudges up. Preoccupied, wet, covered with mud.

> NICK
> Mr Gundy, can I get a ride into town?

> SAM
> What do you need from town, Duke?
> I'll see to it.

> NICK
> I want some time off.

> SAM
> Nobody leaves this Ranch, boy.
> You know the rules.

> CAMILA
> Don't leave us now, Duke.
> You've been doing so well.

                    SAM
         Mr Gundy, you don't need me here.
         You can't grow shrimp in these
         mountains. There's no salt water.

                    SAM
         You need to keep your eyes on the
         BIG VIEW, son. Don't bother me with
         minor details. HERE.

SAM thrusts a 30.06 HUNTING CARBINE at NICK.
NICK looks at it, reluctantly takes it.

                    NICK
         What's this for?

SAM picks up another RIFLE, jumps into the motorized canoe.

                    SAM
         GATORING.
         Happens this time every year.
         Too many of 'em. Gotta thin 'em out.

He loads his rifle.

                    CAMILA
         Oh, please go, Mr Palmer.
         Don't give up now.

NICK looks down at himself, at how dirty he is.
He puts the CARBINE in the boat, pulls off his shirt and dives off the pier.

Swims in a fast crawl out to a small island in the lake, and returns.

NICK heaves himself up into SAM's canoe.

                    NICK
                (to CAMILA)
         Let's go.

SAM laughs and pulls away from the dock.
CAMILA waves goodbye to them.

                    SAM
         My wife's not coming.
         She detests blood sports.

<u>RIVER</u> EXT DAY

NICK and SAM drift slowly through a sea of lilies.

Thick jungle growths drift in the water on both sides.
At times, the jungle plants almost meet overhead.

SAM GUNDY stands in the bow of the dugout canoe.
He grips his 30.06, scanning the water.

NICK sits in the stern.

                    SAM
          Know what the most perfect form is,
          Duke?

                    NICK
               (looking for alligators)
          What... No, Mr Gundy.

                    SAM
          The Triangle is the most perfect form.
          It is the oldest form there is. It was known
          to the Egyptians, to the Druids, to the
          Anasazi, and to the Mayans. The Mayans
          never discovered the wheel, but they
          knew more about the heavens than
          we know today...

He blasts an ALLIGATOR twenty yards away.

                    SAM
          The basis of their science was the
          Triangle. Plus, the three points of
          a Triangle form a Circle.

BANG! He fires at the ALLIGATOR, again.

<u>FURTHER DOWN THE RIVER</u> EXT DAY

They continue to drift.

SAM eyes the water. He lights a cigar.

NICK'S POV – the suggestion of GREEN FACES and BODIES,
moving behind the jungle vines...

                    SAM
          Many a time, smoking a cigar like this,
          I have decided upon the life or death
          of a man. And you know, Duke, I have
          never been bothered by remorse.

                    NICK
          Good for you.

                    SAM
          Why does a man smile to himself as
          he walks down the street? What really
          happens to you when you dream?
          Who's to say when the dream ends?
          Do you ever think about that, Duke?

                    NICK
          Guess I do. Sometimes.

ON THE RIVERBANK

he sees the bodies of the TWO MERCENARIES from the Bunkhouse,
staked out on the ground, full of arrows. Their weapons are scattered
all around.

                    SAM
          If only they could figure out a way to
          eliminate sleep. Me, I hate to dream.
          I always go to bed real late. I'm always
          working, there's so much to do, and
          I'm always the first up in the morning.
          But I still sleep, oh, two, three hours
          every night. Can't seem to get it down.

BANG! BANG! BANG!

SAM fires three shots at the tail of a GATOR.

NICK fires once, deliberately missing.

The GATOR gets away.

                    SAM
          What's the MATTER with you, Duke?
          You haven't hit a GATOR all day.

                    NICK
          I don't know, Mr. Gundy. I guess...

GATORING ain't my thing.

SAM stares hard at NICK. He opens the ICE CHEST.

> SAM
> You're still doing your best, aren't you?

> NICK
> Sure I am.

> SAM
> Lighten up.

He produces Buds.

<u>FURTHER DOWN THE RIVER</u>   EXT   DAY

SAM and NICK crouch in the dugout, bent over their rifles, alert for any
movement beneath the field of lilies. DRINKING MORE BUDS.

> SAM
> A real man doesn't kill for fun, Duke.
> A real man kills for food, or for what's
> right. These GATORS are a menace.
> There are thousands of 'em. Feeding off
> the garbage of the Ranch. They're an
> insult to nature. And every couple
> of months, Duke, they take a native
> child.

> NICK
> Ah, come on, Sam. You love killing 'em.

> SAM
> There are native people living all along
> these banks. Simple savages. They're
> afraid of us. You'll never see one,
> but they're there.

> NICK
> Do you and Camila plan to have a child?

At the mention of CAMILA's name, SAM goes into a minor seizure.
He grabs his head.

THE CANOE BEGINS TO BREAK APART.

WATER gushes up over their feet. The motor sinks.

NICK and SAM dive into the river.

Holding their rifles over their heads, they wade towards the bank.

RIVER BANK   EXT   DAY

SAM and NICK trudge through the thick mud of the river bank.
Impenetrable jungle. Mosquito hordes.

Stepping through the roots of a gigantic tree, they see –

– A BABY.

SAM struggles waist-deep thru the mud and weeds.
He lifts the BABY in his arms.

> SAM
> This is no accident. This is a sign.

> NICK
> Maybe we should look for its... owners.
> Find their village.

> SAM
> Over my dead body. This one's ours.

Cradling the BABY, SAM wades ashore. NICK follows.

JUNGLE PATH   EXT   DAY

SAM and NICK walk down a twisting jungle trail.

SAM croons to the BABY. All around them, HARSH JUNGLE SOUNDS.

LAKESIDE   EXT   DAY

SAM and NICK splash thru weed-clogged, shallow water.

The DOCK is up ahead.

LAKESIDE DOCK   EXT   DAY

They walk up the dock. The KRUGERS are busy carving up the dead sea
animal with CHAINSAWS.

                         MRS KRUGER
               What a beautiful child.

NICK looks at her in horror.

SAM doesn't even hear. He strides towards the –

RANCH EXT DAY

The MILITARY CAMP is in an uproar. Men running everywhere,
jeeps driving up, HELICOPTER setting down.

NICK follows SAM, heading for the BIG HOUSE.

BIG HOUSE EXT DAY

CAMILA storms out to meet them.

                         CAMILA
               All hell has broken loose, Sam.
               That little asshole Smith crossed the
               Border –

                         SAM
               Look what we found. It's a miracle.

                         CAMILA
               Didn't you hear what I said?
               Smith took twenty men and crossed
               the Border. He attacked a town.
               Killed women and children. SAM!
               This is serious. Put that baby down.

                         SAM
               Who knows about this?

                         CAMILA
               Nobody knows. But we've got to
               do something fast.

BRIGGS comes running up.

                    BRIGGS
        It looks bad, Sam. They're pinned
        down ten klicks across the Border.

He hands SAM a walkie-talkie. JOSHUA SMITH can be heard, screaming.

                    SMITH
                 (via radio)
        Help me, please! Help!

SAM holds the BABY and the walkie-talkie.

                    SAM
        Smith, this is Sam Gundy.

                    SMITH
                 (via radio)
        Oh, thank God! You gotta get me
        out of here, Mr Gundy –

                    SAM
        Control yourself, Smith. How many
        men are with you?

                    SMITH
                 (via radio)
        I don't know! Holmes is down,
        and Denby. Ames is hit. Our own
        FRIENDLIES turned against us!

                    SAM
        Do you know your position?
        Do you know where you are?

                    SMITH
                 (via radio)
        AAARGH! AAARGH! AAARGH!

SAM turns the walkie-talkie off. Hands it to BRIGGS.

                    BRIGGS
        The men are all ready, Sam.

                    SAM
        Well, let's get on with it.

SAM tries to hand the BABY to CAMILA.

                    CAMILA
          I don't want that baby.

SAM hands the BABY to NICK. Climbs into a jeep. SUICIDA at the wheel.

                    CAMILA
          Where do you think you're going?

                    SAM
          We'll talk about it after I get back.
                    (to SUICIDA)
          ¡Vamos! ¡Vamos!

                    CAMILA
          Suicida, if you drive away with him,
          you're fired.

                    SAM
          ¡Vamonos! ¡Vamonos!

SUICIDA, confused and frightened, guns the motor but does not
engage the gears.

                    CAMILA
          Listen, Sam. You're flipping out.
          The Ranch is falling apart and instead
          of dealing with it you're running off
          to get involved in someone else's
          problem.

                    SAM
          It's my problem, too. These are my
          own men. They'd do the same for me.

                    CAMILA
          They disobeyed your orders! They
          waited till your back was turned,
          and then they went and fucked up!
          They betrayed you, Sam. Let them
          take the consequences.

SAM is silent, obviously moved by her argument.

                    CAMILA
                    (low-voiced)
          Sam, Hector is being killed today.
          This whole thing is going to blow up.
          You must stay on the Ranch.

                    BRIGGS
          Sam, we're all ready if you are.
          There's not a man here, sir, that
          wouldn't follow you to hell and back.
          Your men need you.

SAM and CAMILA exchange a long look.

                    SAM
          I have no choice.

SAM jams the jeep into gear. SUICIDA jolts forward, drives away.
BRIGGS follows in the Land Rover.

NICK trails after CAMILA into the –

BIG HOUSE INT DAY

CAMILA, shaking with fury, strides to the bar and pours herself a stiff shot
of rum. She drinks it straight down and hurls the glass at the framed photo
of SAM with BIGELOW and the FLAG.

The glass shatters the photograph.

NICK hovers in the doorway, holding the BABY.

                    NICK
          Ahem... uh... Miz Gundy, Ma'am.
          What shall I do with THIS?

                    CAMILA
          Do what you want with it.
          It's not one of *my* problems.

NICK puts the BABY down on the sofa. He crosses over to CAMILA.
She turns away from him.

                    NICK
          You're upset, aren't you?

                    CAMILA
          I am never upset.

                    NICK
          Let me help you.

                    CAMILA
          I don't need your help.

                    NICK
          Let me help you in your loneliness.

                    CAMILA
          I'm not lonely. And I'm not upset.
          Get out of here. And take that baby
          with you.

NICK doesn't move.

                    NICK
          I was kind of hoping I could use your
          shower.

                    CAMILA
          Aren't you going out to FIGHT?

They look through the window at the preparations for battle.
SAM directs his troops beside the HELICOPTER.

                    NICK
          I prefer to take a shower.

                    CAMILA
          Suit yourself.

She exits, leaving NICK staring out the window. The BABY starts to cry.

MILITARY CAMP EXT DAY

SAM stands beside the chopper, poring over maps with BRIGGS.
The TROOPS wait in landcruisers and jeeps.

                    SAM
          We'll go ahead and call in their
          position. We shall engage the
          enemy within the hour.

He boards the HELICOPTER. All the other vehicles pull away along the
muddy road. The chopper takes off.

HELICOPTER INT DAY

SAM sits with BRIGGS and GUNTHER. BRIGGS cleans his weapon, meticulous, tense. GUNTHER is placid, singing to himself.

> PILOT
> ¡Humo! ¡Humo a la derecha!

> GUNTHER
> Smoke! Up on the right!

FOREST   EXT   DAY

TWO LOCALS clad in camouflage aim a jerry-rigged MISSILE LAUNCHER at the HELICOPTER overhead.

We have seen these guys before – working on SAM GUNDY's Ranch.

THWAP! A HEAT-SEEKING MISSILE hurtles towards the chopper.

IN THE AIR

The MISSILE misses the body of the HELICOPTER –

– slices thru the TAIL ROTOR BLADES –

HELICOPTER   INT   DAY

The craft shudders violently, starts to spiral downwards, OUT OF CONTROL.

All except SAM GUNDY panic.

> SAM
> Keep calm! Keep calm!

SUDDENLY THE CHOPPER IS FILLED WITH BLUISH LIGHT.

The craft stops falling. It is suspended in mid-air. The MEN scream. A beatific smile plays across SAM's face.

The LIGHT grows in intensity. The MEN fall silent, awed.

SAM continues to smile. WHITE OUT.

JUNGLE TRAIL   EXT   DAY

FADE IN FROM WHITE –

SAM GUNDY stands on a trail in the jungle.

BRIGGS, GUNTHER, SUICIDA and the rest are scattered around him.
They still have their weapons. No sign of the HELICOPTER.

All look around, amazed.

                    GUNTHER
          What happened to the – ?

                    SAM
          Move out, men. No time to waste.

GUNFIRE in the immediate vicinity. The voice of SMITH is heard.

                    SMITH
          Help me! For God's sake, someone
          help me! Please!

SAM gives a signal to his MEN. They deploy into the jungle.

JUNGLE CLEARING EXT DAY

SMITH, AMES and four surviving MERCENARIES are pinned down in a clearing.
The MEN of SMITH's force lie dead around them. Cacophony of gunfire.

SAM and his TROOPS reach the clearing.

They spot the GUERRILLAS who have SMITH pinned down.

The GUERRILLAS have their backs to them.

SAM and his MEN open fire.

BIG HOUSE BATHROOM INT DAY

NICK emerges from a cloud of steam. He wraps himself in a white towel.
Looks around for his clothes.

They are gone. All he can find is a t-shirt.

The t-shirt says, KILL 'EM ALL – LET GOD SORT 'EM OUT.

He puts it on.

<u>BEDROOM</u> INT DAY

NICK enters, wearing t-shirt and towel.

CAMILA sits upright in a stiff-backed chair. Browsing a TRAVEL MAGAZINE.

                    NICK
          Have you seen my pants, Miz Gundy?

                    CAMILA
          I threw them out. They were too dirty
          to be washed.

She rises, crosses to NICK.

The cut of her dress reveals her extraordinary figure.

                    CAMILA
          And anyway, you won't be needing them.

They kiss passionately. NICK loses his towel.

<u>JUNGLE CLEARING</u> EXT DAY

SAM and his MEN have won the day.

The LOCALS are apparently all dead. Though fewer in number, SAM'S TROOPS
have taken the enemy by surprise, completely routing them.

SAM attends to AMES, who is severely wounded.

SMITH crouches in his foxhole, jabbering incoherently.

                    SMITH
          Help me – I'm hit – in pain –

BRIGGS brings in SIX PRISONERS, bound with razor wire. They are Rama
Indians. They speak only their native dialect. They wear camouflage.
Proud and ready to die.

                    BRIGGS
          What shall I do with these?

                    GUNTHER
          Get rid of them.

                    BRIGGS
          Okay by me.
                    (produces his RAMBO KNIFE)
          Cut me a few ears first –

                    SAM
          Release those men.

                    BRIGGS
          Are you kidding? They're the enemy.

                    SAM
          You heard me. I said cut 'em loose.

                    BRIGGS
          YOU'RE CRAZY! FUCK YOU, GUNDY!
          I AIN'T GONNA –

                    SAM
          Do as I say.

BRIGGS staggers, as if bashed between the eyes. For a moment, he loses control
of his arms and legs, as if in epileptic seizure.

Dazed, he starts cutting the PRISONERS loose.

                    SMITH
          Help me! Please! Somebody please
          help me!

SAM notices SMITH. He glances at SUICIDA.

                    SAM
          Why don't you help him out?

SUICIDA unholsters his PISTOL. He marches up to SMITH and shoots him
several times.

AMES calls feebly out to SAM.

                    AMES
          I'm finished, Sam. Help me out, too.

SAM cradles AMES in his arms.

                    SAM
          You can't die, Ames. You're my neighbor.

AMES shakes his head. His eyes roll back –

SAM stares at him intently. AMES' eyes pop forward again.
He rises, as if pulled by a magnetic force.

One of the PRISONERS pulls a knife out of his shirt.
He hurls the knife at SAM.

THE KNIFE sticks deep in SAM's back.

SAM looks around and sees the knife. He feels no pain. He barely bleeds.
HE PULLS THE KNIFE OUT OF HIS BACK, and rises.

SAM approaches the PRISONER who threw the knife. The INDIAN stares
at him, astounded. SAM hands the knife back to the PRISONER.

SAM speaks to the INDIAN in his native tongue. The PRISONER answers.
SAM addresses the other INDIANS.

The INDIANS confer, nod their agreement, and disappear into the forest.

>   SAM
>   Let's get back to the Ranch.

POOLSIDE, RANCH EXT NIGHT

NICK and CAMILA float inside inflated rubber animals.

They drink Cuba Libres. CAMILA wears her bathing suit.
NICK wears SAM's trunks, and smokes one of his cigars.

The BABY sleeps on a pool lounger.

Mosquitoes and moths crackle and burn on the Electric Insect Killer.

LIGHTNING.

>   NICK
>   This sure is the life, Miz Gundy.

>   CAMILA
>   I prefer you not call me Miz Gundy
>   any more. Call me Camila again.

>   NICK
>   Well, I don't rightly know that I can

do that, MIZ GUNDY –

                    CAMILA
          I could fall in love with you if you
          weren't such an asshole.

                    NICK
          You could?

                    CAMILA
          Yes. I could.

                    NICK
          When Sam gets back, I guess he'll
          shoot me. Maybe he'll shoot us both.

                    CAMILA
          No, he won't, because he'll never know.
          In half an hour you'll be in the Bunkhouse
          and I'll be back in my room.

                    NICK
          I'm never going back to the Bunkhouse.
          I'm gonna lay here and work on my tan.

HEADLIGHTS sweep around the side of the Big House.
For a moment, NICK and CAMILA are blinded.

BIGELOW'S MERCEDES pulls up beside the pool. Another Merc and several
jeeps with ARMED GUARDS draw up alongside.

BIGELOW emerges from the car. He is followed by shady characters in SUITS.

                    BIGELOW
          Good evening, Mrs Gundy. Sorry to
          disturb you, but WHERE'S SAM?

                    CAMILA
          My husband... didn't you see him?
          He's outside somewhere. Prowling
          around the Ranch. Duke! Fix Mr
          Bigelow and his friends some drinks.

NICK climps out of his inflated animal. Heads for the bar beside the pool.

                    BIGELOW
          Mrs Gundy, it is my sad duty to inform
          you that Hector Cruz has been

assassinated.

CAMILA feigns surprise.

> CAMILA
> You don't say.

> BIGELOW
> Somebody bombed his press conference.
> American journalists are dead.
> The American Ambassador is injured.
> Fingers are being pointed. I must speak
> to Sam right away.

> CAMILA
> You really fucked up, didn't you, Wort?

One of the SUITS steps forward.

> SUIT 1
> It's very important that we speak to Mr
> Gundy. So that we can help him.

> SUIT 2
> Many people think your husband is
> responsible.

> CAMILA
> Why would they think that? Wort,
> are you trying to set him up?

> BIGELOW
> My name is not Wort. It's Worth.

> CAMILA
> Sorry. My mistake.

NICK presents BIGELOW with a Cuba Libre. Emboldened by rum and lustful
romance, NICK stands one inch from BIGELOW's face.

> NICK
> You got a lot of balls, Charlie.
> Barging into a man's home and
> charging him with MURDER.
> Specially when he's been out
> FIGHTING TERRORISTS all day!

> BIGELOW

What? Where the hell is he?

                    NICK
          Across the Border. Deep in hostile
          territory. Killing communists and
          saving American lives.

BIGELOW turns pale green. He grabs the back of the pool lounger,
nearly tipping the BABY into the water.

                    NICK
          Careful with the baby, mister.

BIGELOW turns his back on them, heads for the house.

                    BIGELOW
          I must use the phone!

With much shouting and slamming of doors, MEN and VEHICLES follow
BIGELOW into the BIG HOUSE.

NICK, CAMILA and the BABY are alone.

                    NICK
          Looks like your husband's caught
          between a rock and a hard place.

                    CAMILA
          That's for sure.

                    NICK
          Camila. Now's the time that Sam
          needs us. Needs you, especially.
          We must stand behind him.

                    CAMILA
          Do you think so?

                    NICK
          Yeah. I do.

                    CAMILA
          Well, I don't. I think Sam's gone mad,
          and things are finished here.

                    NICK
          You do?

                    CAMILA
          Yes. I do.

                    NICK
          ALL RIGHT! LET'S GO!

He helps her out of the pool. They head for the Big House.

JUNGLE EXT NIGHT

SAM GUNDY stands upright in a jeep, bouncing along the jungle trail.

AMES, GUNTHER, BRIGGS and the SURVIVORS ride behind him.
AMES examines his wounds. There are none.

                    AMES
          Jesus, Briggs. I feel great!
          I haven't felt this good in 30 years!

LIGHTNING.

HIGH VIEW OF RANCH LANDS EXT NIGHT

A FIELD OF LIGHTNING plays over the jungle, moving toward the Ranch.

The RED MUSTANG travels in the opposite direction.

MUSTANG INT NIGHT

CAMILA drives. NICK is her passenger.

NICK wears one of SAM's hideous checkered sport coats, SAM's western
shirt and Stetson hat. He and CAMILA are deliriously happy.

                    CAMILA
          In two nights, we'll be in Guatemala
          City. I have two sisters there. One of
          them is very rich. She has a beach
          house where we can stay for nothing.

                    NICK
          Do they have cable?

                    CAMILA
          They have everything.

                    NICK
          How about a refrigerator?

                    CAMILA
          They have a walk-in freezer, Duke.
          And it is full of frozen steaks and
          ice-cold beer. And in the video are
          X-rated movies, Duke, and football
          games. They have everything.

                    NICK
          I don't need anything as long as
          I have you.

RANCH   EXT   NIGHT

The BABY lies beside the pool.

An INDIAN COUPLE dressed in blankets and serapes emerge from the night.
The WOMAN grabs the CHILD.

From her expression, it is obvious that this is her BABY.

The sound of engines. Jeep headlights sweep across them.
The COUPLE and the BABY disappear.

BIG HOUSE   EXT   NIGHT

SAM GUNDY'S CONVOY screeches to a halt among BIGELOW'S MEN.
SAM marches straight for the –

BIG ROOM   INT   NIGHT

The SUITS sit around drinking coffee and going through SAM's private files.
BIGELOW is on the phone.

                    BIGELOW
          That's right, sir. Millions of dollars
          unaccounted for. We have all the
          evidence right here. Yes, sir,
          I'm sure we can hang everything
          on him – the assassination, too.
          No problem –

SAM enters. BIGELOW hangs up.

> BIGELOW
> Sam! Are you okay? How was your
> mission? Did you find Smith?

> SAM
> Who are these people?

> BIGELOW
> Our people, Sam. This is Mr Martinez
> from the D.I.S. Mr Thorpe from State.
> Mr Walters, Mr Donahue.
> (aside)
> You and I must go to Washington.

SAM notices the picture of himself and BIGELOW in D.C., with its glass smashed.

> SAM
> What for?

> BIGELOW
> There's a flap on. Hector Cruz is dead.
> The op went wrong. Ambassador
> got shot. You and I need to go to
> Washington and smooth the waters.

> SAM
> That's not the way it's gonna be.

THUNDER.

SAM sees LITTLE SAM and CRYSTAL coming down the stairs with suitcases.

> SAM
> Where do you kids think you're going?
> It's after your curfew.

> CRYSTAL
> Spring break's over, Dad. I'm going
> back to school.

> LITTLE SAM
> I'm going, too, Dad. Gotta get my band
> together.

> SAM
> That's good, Crystal.

Little Sam, you're staying here.

                    LITTLE SAM
          No way, Pops. Fuck y –

LITTLE SAM is wracked by a seizure.
He falls speechless to his knees.

                    BIGELOW
          What's going on here?

                    SAM
          Family matters.
          None of your concern.

                    BIGELOW
          Throw a few things in a suitcase, Sam.
          We must catch the first available plane.

                    SAM
          Where is my wife?

CRYSTAL bolts from the room, carrying her bags.
SAM concentrates on LITTLE SAM, still on his knees.

                    LITTLE SAM
          She left – a couple hours ago –
          with Duke Palmer.

SAM is frozen, staring down.

BIGELOW and the SUITS close in. Pulling their guns –

                    BIGELOW
          I don't want it to come to this, Sam.
          But I must insist –

SAM looks around. He seems to be TALLER.

                    SAM
          Still here?

                    BIGELOW
          Sam, I'm replacing you. You're no
          longer a team player. There's been
          too much messing up around here.
          Someone must take responsibility.
          I'm ordering you OFF THE RANCH.

SAM's mind is obviously elsewhere. He seems TALLER STILL.

                         SAM
              Ranch... What ranch?

                        SUIT 2
              Mr Bigelow!

The SUIT points at SAM GUNDY's feet.

SAM has LEVITATED two feet off the ground.

The hardwood floor below him is ablaze.

SAM GUNDY laughs, and seizes BIGELOW, lifting him up off the ground.

SAM TEARS BIGELOW APART.

BIG HOUSE EXT NIGHT

The sound of GUNSHOTS within.

CHILLING SCREAMS are heard.

AMES, BRIGGS and GUNTHER stare in horror at the House. They cannot move.

SAN CARLOS   EXT DAWN

The streets are muddy. No one is about.

San Carlos now seems the most relaxed place in the world.

NICK and CAMILA stop beside the LITTLE SHRINE where NICK stashed
his I.D.s. NICK retrieves them.

He does not show them to CAMILA. They drive on.

MUSTANG INT DAY

NICK drives. CAMILA's head rests on his shoulder.

                        CAMILA
              Do you have any regrets, Duke?

                    NICK
          No. Well, there were a few things I left
          unfinished. But I've forgotten what
          they were. I love you, Camila.

                    CAMILA
          I love you, too, Nick. Very much.
          What kind of things?

                    NICK
          Oh... what's right and what's wrong.
          And what to do about it.
          Nothing important.

MUSTANG INT NIGHT

She drives. He tries to stay awake. She chews gum and blows bubbles.

                    CAMILA
          Why don't you climb in the back?
          Get some sleep.

                    NICK
          No, that's all right. I can't sleep
          anyway. You're gum's keeping me
          awake.
                    (a silence)
          What are you thinking about?

                    CAMILA
          Somebody told me once never to ask
          that question.

                    NICK
          Why?

                    CAMILA
          Because they might tell you.

                    NICK
          Well... what are you thinking about?

                    CAMILA
          I'm thinking about Sam.

She continues chewing, popping bubbles.

<u>MUSTANG</u> INT DAY

NICK drives. Obvious tension between him and CAMILA.

>   CAMILA
> How much money do we have left?

>   NICK
> About fifty dollars. We'll have to
> use your credit cards.

>   CAMILA
> The only credit cards I have are Sam's.
> I wouldn't feel right using them.

>   NICK
> You're so FULL OF SHIT. You're running
> out on Sam and you're worried about
> his credit cards. We can go anywhere
> in the world. RIO.

>   CAMILA
> I hate Rio.

>   NICK
> Tokyo, then. Melbourne. Bombay.
> Switzerland.

>   CAMILA
> Duke, you are *estupido.* Those are
> the worst places in the world. You
> have no taste and no real feelings.

>   NICK
> I know. How about Santa Fe?

<u>ROADSIDE</u> EXT DAY

The MUSTANG is pulled off the road.
The rear wheel is jacked up.

CAMILA changes the tire. NICK sulks.

A sign says, CIUDAD DE GUATEMALA 20 KM.

>   CAMILA

I hate making mistakes like this.
I wish I'd never left the Ranch!

                    NICK
Yeah? Well, I wish I'd never left, too!
Sam was the first person that ever
treated me STRAIGHT! And I
betrayed him.

She finishes with the tire, lets down the jack. Rolls the flat tire into a ditch.

                    CAMILA
Are you crazy? Sam doesn't even
know your name. You're just one of
the assholes from the Bunkhouse.

                    NICK
Sam had PLANS for me! He was
going to make me FOREMAN!
And I gave it all up for love. Well,
fuck that!

The look at each other. Look around.

                    CAMILA
I want to go home, Nick.

                    NICK
              (opening the car door)
Be my guest.

They get in. CAMILA peels out, heading back the way they came.

MUSTANG INT DAY

CAMILA drives fast thru the mountains. NICK is puzzled.

                    NICK
Why did you call me Nick?

                    CAMILA
I don't know. I must have been
thinking of someone else.

MOUNTAIN ROAD EXT DUSK

The MUSTANG speeds back towards the Ranch.

LIGHTNING. THUNDER.

<u>SAM GUNDY'S RANCH</u> EXT NIGHT

Lightning flickers in the sky.

CAMILA drives up the road to the Big House.

Jeeps and Mercedes Benz are parked as before, headlights burning, engines running.

AMES, BRIGGS, GUNTHER and SUICIDA are frozen in the positions in which we last saw them.

All staring wide-eyed at the Big House.

NICK and CAMILA climb out of the car.

> CAMILA
> Briggs, Ames. What are you doing?
> Gunther! Suicida!

None of them reply. All remain frozen.

> CAMILA
> Something terrible is happening.

> NICK
> We must go in.

He marches toward the front door.

> CAMILA
> No!

> NICK
> We must!

<u>BIG HOUSE</u> INT NIGHT

The hall is filled with eerie light.

The Big Door opens. NICK and CAMILA slide in.

They hear a strange sound like HUGE HISSING COCKROACHES rushing
past their feet and buzzing overhead.

But there is nothing there. They approach the –

BIG ROOM INT NIGHT

In darkness, save for the PHOSPHORESCENT GLOW that emanates
from SAM GUNDY.

SAM weighs 1200 lbs. He is shaped like a PYRAMID.

He hovers, six feet off the ground.

BIGELOW and his MEN are masses of jelly on the floor. Without skeletons,
yet still alive. Their faces are grotesque shapeless masks with staring eyes.

CAMILA and NICK enter the big room.

SAM smiles benignly.

NICK freezes, stunned.

CAMILA takes a few steps further into the room.
She stares at the remains of BIGELOW.

                    CAMILA
          Sam, that's disgusting. It's EVIL.

                    SAM
          That's a matter of opinion.

The FORMS disappear.

                    CAMILA
          What did you do with them?

                    SAM
          Storage.

                    NICK
          We shouldn't have come back.

                    SAM
          You had no choice.

SAM's voice rumbles back and forth across the room, like THUNDER.

                    CAMILA
          What's the matter with you, Sam?
          Why are you doing this?

                    SAM
          I'm doing it for us, Camila. For all three
          of us. What do you say, Nick?
          Are you ready for the NEXT STEP?

                    NICK
          I'm with you, Sam. Same as always.

CAMILA looks down and sees NICK'S FEET are floating six inches off the ground.

                    CAMILA
          Nick! Get down from there!
                  (to SAM)
          I don't know what this is all about
          but it had BETTER STOP!

                    SAM
          You don't want it to stop, Camila.
          You want to be part of it.

                    CAMILA
          Bullshit! Nick, don't listen to him!
          He's trying to CONTROL YOUR MIND!
          NICK!

NICK is gone. Floating a foot above the floor, staring into SAM GUNDY'S
PULSATING THIRD EYE.

                    SAM
          I'm going thru some kind of change.
          I can't explain it because I don't fully
          understand. It has to do with ALIEN
          INTELLIGENCE and the HISTORICAL
          POSITION OF THE RANCH. I am
          becoming something BETTER.
          But I can't make the next step alone.

                    CAMILA
          Are you an ALIEN, Sam?

A BOLT OF LIGHTING flashes up and hits one of SAM's lower corners.
The lightning flickers around the room.

The sound of RUSHING COCKROACHES is heard again.
The SHADOW OF THEIR WINGS is seen.

                         SAM
              I don't know what I am.
              But I know what I can become.
              You and Nick have to join me so that
              we can move to the NEXT LEVEL –

                         CAMILA
              Oh, Sam. That's so pathetic.
              The answer's no.

SAM's floating pyramid rotates. SAM has three faces, all speaking at once.

                         SAM
              You don't understand, Camila –
              Three is the evolutionary number –
              The number of unity –
              Body, mind and spirit –
              Not two by two shall we enter the
              FUTURE ARK –
              But THREE BY THREE!

MORE LIGHTNING. SOUND OF ROCKET ENGINES.

NICK – his mind entirely in the power of SAM – experiences SAM'S VISION.

Thru his POV we see THE THREE OF THEM

-- walking hand-in-hand through a verdant landscape –

– underwater swimming with dolphins –

– standing on the rocky moon of an UNKNOWN PLANET, staring at the
LIGHTS OF CITIES burning on the planet's darkened side –

<u>BIG ROOM</u> INT NIGHT

CAMILA stamps her foot. She tugs at NICK's pants leg.

                         CAMILA
              Bullshit. This is all your trip, Sam.
              Heads you win, tails we lose.

                         SAM
              Camila, please. Together we can rise

                    above this. We can become HIGHER
                    POWERS. We will be like GODS.

                              CAMILA
                    It all sounds great, Sam. Except
                    for one thing. I don't love you.

SAM grimaces. His faces seem smaller.

CAMILA drags NICK back to the floor. He receives a mild electric shock.
He shakes his head.

                              SAM
                    Camila – please – this isn't just for
                    me – this is for all of us –

A WIND BLOWS UP. SAM is shrinking fast.

                              SAM
                    I CAN DESTROY YOU!!!

                              CAMILA
                    No, you can't. You're far too
                    sentimental.

CAMILA pushes NICK thru the Big Door.

She glances back. SAM is engulfed by LIGHTNING.

RANCH EXT NIGHT

Overhead, THREE LIGHTS form a TRIANGLE in the sky.

CAMILA and NICK jump in the Mustang. It does not start.

BIG ROOM INT DAY

SAM's three faces are contorted with pain. His cheeks collapse.
His whole body is collapsing.

WIND and whirling debris fill the room.

RANCH EXT NIGHT

The Big House grows darker and darker. LIGHTNING.

CAMILA tries to start the car. The motor flickers, faintly.

BIG ROOM INT NIGHT

SAMA is two feet tall, still shrinking, screaming.

RANCH EXT NIGHT

The Mustang starts up. CAMILA puts the car in gear. It roars away.

AMES, GUNTHER, BRIGGS and the REST are still frozen,
staring at the HOUSE.

The HOUSE itself is getting smaller. All the windows break.

MUSTANG INT NIGHT

CAMILA's foot is all the way down on the pedal.
They speed through the night.

A BRILLIANT FLASH BEHIND THEM.

RANCH EXT NIGHT

The Big House disappears in a NUCLEAR BLAST.

All the BUILDINGS, VEHICLES, and MERCENARIES are SUCKED UP
INTO THE INFERNO.

The THREE LIGHTS are gone.

A GLOWING ORANGE MUSHROOM FILLS THE SKY.

MOUNTAINS EXT NIGHT

The Mustang speeds on, down a winding mountain road.

THE MUSHROOM CLOUD rises behind it.

MUSTANG INT DAWN

CAMILA and NICK drive into the SUNRISE.

SAM'S SPELL is broken, and they are IN LOVE again.

<u>MOUNTAIN ROAD</u>   EXT   DAWN

The Mustang crests a rise and greets the dawn.

The MOUNTAINS are wreathed in clouds, glistening with dew.

Everything ahead of them is fresh and unspoiled.

                         NICK
            Do you still have his CREDIT CARDS?

                    THE END

Cox/Wurlitzer 1: *Body Parts*

by James Kenney

They met in a bar in Rotterdam. Harry Dean Stanton made the introduction.

Alex Cox had come to town to screen *Repo Man*, which he had written and directed, featuring Stanton in a rare lead alongside unknown Emilio Estevez. Stanton, a character actor legend, all quiet presence, no pretense, was having a drink with a bearded man he introduced as "Rudy."

"You must be Rudy Wurlitzer!" exclaimed Cox, an avid admirer. Two days later, Wurlitzer lent Cox a hundred dollars to cover his hotel phone bill. Then Cox went off to make *Walker* and asked Wurlitzer to come along and write it.

Cox was a young British director with a sharp wit shaped by punk and provocation. Wurlitzer was a more seasoned American novelist who drifted into screenwriting almost sideways. What they shared was a taste for disruption. Wurlitzer wrote *Two-Lane Blacktop* in 1971, directed by Monte Hellman, a film featured on the cover of *Esquire* magazine, which declared it another *Easy Rider*. The film was quickly assigned the outsider classic status it still rightly holds today, but wasn't a commercial success. Similarly, after being prematurely consigned to home video, *Repo Man* clawed its way back into theatrical circulation.

By the end of the decade, the two had partnered up for a combustible creative period of collaboration, the first part documented by *Walker*, which (sounds familiar) was resoundingly rejected on release only to earn its status as a brave, crazy, political classic in the coming years. This was followed by two equally brave, muscular screenplays that were quite filmable but also quite flammable. The money stayed away. With this book you can see what should have been the next step in a most productive creative partnership.

To understand Cox and Wurlitzer, it helps to step back and see Cox and Wurlitzer first as separate forces.

Cox was born in England in 1954. He dropped out of law school. Film was his passion, and UCLA followed. That outsider position—a Brit loose in late-1970s Hollywood—sharpened both Cox's fascination with America and his irreverent view of American pop culture and politics. He exploded in the mid-1980s with two cult hits the *Los Angeles Times* described as "nihilist fantasy" (*Repo Man*, 1984) and a "punk valentine" (*Sid & Nancy*, 1986). The dichotomy of these terms nicely sums up Cox's work: dark and humanistic. The films had little in common on the surface. One was a surreal science fiction comedy about Los Angeles repo men and alien conspiracies; the other a bruising account of Sid Vicious and Nancy Spungen's mutual destruction culminating in a murder-suicide in New York's Chelsea Hotel.

If Cox's career has proved a manifesto of sorts, *Repo Man* is page one. It is scrappy and unhinged and strangely prophetic. Former Monkee Michael Nesmith persuaded Universal to finance the film, which upon release came and went. Then it came back. The soundtrack circulated. Home video did what it did sometimes in the 1980s with quality work that slipped through the cracks: it gave a second life. What began as an overlooked B-movie became a midnight movie fixture, running for eighteen months at a downtown New York movie house and eventually grossing $4 million. Today *Repo Man* is canon. Its one-liners ("Let's go get sushi and not pay") still shows up on unauthorized t-shirts, and its genre collision of rowdy humor, government paranoia, and repo culture, with Reagan-era dread humming underneath, make it endure. Punk and humor render the dread not only survivable, but enjoyable.

Sid & Nancy followed. The film takes a self-destructive romance seriously, even when it's absurd. The generally disagreeable John Lydon of the Sex Pistols objected, calling the film "the lowest form of life." Audiences and critics disagreed. The film proved that Cox could balance the punk aggression already present with *Repo Man* with surprisingly delicate emotional fragility.

He could have followed *Sid & Nancy*'s financial and critical success with something a little more, well—*commercial*. That is generally what's done after Hollywood sits up and takes notice of good reviews and good box office. Instead, Cox made the personal lark *Straight to Hell*, a cheerfully, bafflingly absurd Spaghetti Western with Joe Strummer, Courtney Love and half the Pogues, shot in Spain. Janet Maslin in the *New York Times* wrote that Cox was "clearly a director of great promise" but felt the film was "one long private joke." (She's not entirely wrong. Cox is a lover of Spaghetti Westerns and wrote a great book about them.)

Cox turned down *RoboCop 2* and other films around this time, which from one angle is a great shame. He was actually an inspired choice, certainly by Hollywood hiring terms. Cox had, after all, already made his own Reagan-era science fiction parable about men who serve capitalism at the expense of their own humanity, much like Verhoeven's original *Robocop*. *RoboCop 2* might have worked with Cox at the helm, but the producers of a sequel were more interested in mayhem than message. This was not, by Cox's own measure, his territory.

Then came *Walker*, his boldest film, which also proved the end of his studio career. Some got it right away. Vincent Canby in the *New York Times* described it as a "hip, cool, political satire" that was "something very rare in American movies... it has some nerve." By the mid-1980s, Cox had become deeply interested in Nicaragua and its revolution. The story of William Walker, a nineteenth-century American mercenary who invaded Nicaragua and crowned himself president, was, for Cox, almost providentially suited to his purposes. At the time, Reagan had gotten America neck-deep into Nicaragua, and here was the story of an American who openly seized it for himself in the 1850s, as the United States looked the other way. To write the screenplay, Cox enlisted Rudy Wurlitzer.

If Cox was punk cinema's provocateur, Rudy Wurlitzer was Hollywood's literary outlaw. He was born in 1937, scion of a diminishing Wurlitzer instrument fortune, but walked away from comfort early. He ran off to sea at 17, working on an oil tanker to Morocco and Kuwait. He drifted through revolutionary Cuba. He spent time in Paris in the 1960s, then landed in New York's East Village, where he fell in with Robert Frank (whom he later directed *Candy Mountain* with, which Jonathan Rosenbaum called "a wry, laid back *Heart of Darkness*"), Claes Oldenburg, Philip Glass—people for whom disruption was a working method.

His first novel, *Nog*, came out in 1968. Reviewers reached for Pynchon, which was reasonable enough, though Wurlitzer was after something quieter, I'd posit. Rosenbaum argues that Wurlitzer was applying "the lessons of Beckett to the meaning of his own experience." *Flats* and *Quake* followed, in 1970 and 1974. Mood mattered more than momentum, consciousness over plot. Wurlitzer later said he was "trying to explore the composition of the self and what's real and what isn't." The opposite of three-act screenplay logic.

Filmmakers noticed. Monte Hellman read *Nog* and hired Wurlitzer to write *Two-Lane Blacktop* (1971). The resulting road movie is spare and resistant, more poem than plot. It failed spectacularly on release. That part is often forgotten, rightfully, and over time *Two-Lane Blacktop* found its audience anyway. Wurlitzer's reputation grew with it.

Pat Garrett & Billy the Kid followed in 1973, for Sam Peckinpah. Another outlaw, making another production chewed up by the studio before it reached theaters. Even in the initially released version Peckinpah didn't intend, the script still reads as unmistakably Wurlitzer: elegiac, unhurried, more interested in what men carry around inside of them than in what they do. His work continued to move between page and screen. That movement culminated in the unproduced *Slow Fade* (1984), based on his own novel about a filmmaker that may or may not be Peckinpah, which Cox would later call "one of the best scripts I have ever read."

So now we're back to the point where they met in a bar with Harry Dean watching, an unpaid phone bill, and the formation of a creative partnership. Their working process was fluid, unpretentious, and apparently enjoyable. "We worked all kinds of ways," Cox explains. "Rudy wrote *Walker* entirely on his own, though there were several drafts and he incorporated many changes. Afterwards we would work together in a motel room in Tucson, one of us at the Selectric II keyboard, the other pacing." Sometimes Wurlitzer would vanish and return with pages, sometimes pages would arrive by fax from wherever he was. Cox understood his own role clearly: structural rather than literary. "My contribution to our process was that no scene should be longer than three pages." Characters, texture, momentum—those belonged to Wurlitzer. "Rudy made the story work and put flesh on those bones."

Regarding *Body Parts*, Cox explains, "When Rudy and I were in Nicaragua, the Central American press had many stories about *secuestradores*, who would kidnap and murder children and ship their body parts to the first world for transplant purposes." Traveling through Mexico only reinforced the horror. "The Mexican papers would have stories about *sacaojos*—eye stealers—who stole poor people's body parts and shipped them to the U.S., Europe, and the Middle East." In the Western media, Cox noted, "this story went untold." So they decided to write a script about it. "How could such things be? Was it a fantasy?" Years later, the international organ trade was exposed and grimly validated. Stephen Frears made a film about it, *Dirty Pretty Things*. Cox and Wurlitzer had gotten there first, in the desert, at the Selectric II.

The project attracted serious actors. Stanton, who had starred in *Repo Man*, was up for it, "until he wasn't." Cox and Wurlitzer then met Rip Torn. "The perfect actor to play Detective Ditko!" Cox also met with Rose McGowan, and imagined Kirk Douglas as the film's Mad Doctor. Behind the scenes, producer Lorenzo O'Brien, who had produced *Walker* and was, in Cox's words, "the best producer we knew," traveled to Tucson, scouted locations, and budgeted and scheduled the project, fully prepared to move forward.

The film stalled anyway. "Actors tended to like our scripts," says Cox. "Unfortunately, financiers prefer movie stars to actors."

Body Parts exists in the narrow gap between artistic conviction and an industry unwilling to bankroll material that was politically radioactive and commercially unassured. They had developed the project for nearly a year with Zenith, the English company that had made *Sid & Nancy*—totally legitimate, Cox recalls, but saddled with an American partner who never could come up with the money. Eventually O'Brien shut down the Tucson office and returned to Los Angeles. Wurlitzer went back to New York. Cox stayed on a few extra days to close things out.

On his last afternoon, he drove his Chevy Impala out to Gates Pass for a sunset stroll. Heading back into town, he came upon a car—upside down, leaking gas into the road. Its driver had dropped her cigarette and, struggling to find it, had overturned the car on the sharply-curving road. Cox and a passing biker stopped. He lent her his Swiss Army knife to cut herself free. They led the disoriented driver to shelter.

Then her car exploded.

"All agreed," Cox notes, "that it wasn't much of an explosion. Not like in the movies, where there's a loud bang and the car leaps into the air. But more than enough to do her in. So some good came of the *Body Parts* saga, after all."

BODY PARTS

by RUDY WURLITZER
and ALEX COX

copyright 2016

<u>DOWNTOWN TUCSON</u>   EXT   NIGHT

TITLE: ARIZONA   1989

DETECTIVES spread eagle three SUSPECTS against a wall.

COP CARS with flashing lights block the street.

DEPT OF PUBLIC SAFETY OFFICERS RICHARDSON and ORTEGA are tearing apart a van. On its side is a distinctive mural of Saguaros, Zapata and the Virgin Mary.

Uniformed COPS direct traffic and set flares.

DETECTIVES JACK DITKO and BOB BAXTER, partners for ten years, are dressed like bums.

JACK wears a dirty straw cowboy hat. He has sleepless eyes and several days' growth of bear.

BAXTER presses his gun into a SUSPECT's chin while JACK handcuffs the other two.

> BAXTER
> Digame, pendejo! Donde esta Quintana?

> SUSPECT's
> No se, jefe.

JACK reads the SUSPECTS their rights.

> JACK
> You have the right to remain silent.
> Anything you say may be taken down and
> used as evidence against you in a court of
> law. You have the right to a lawyer. If you
> cannot afford a lawyer –

> SUSPECT
> Hey, Ditko. These cuffs are too tight –

JACK loosens the cuffs.

BAXTER, enraged by the silence of the THIRD SUSPECT, punches him in the kidneys. The MAN falls down.

> BAXTER
> Don't like to me, asshole.

                    JACK
              Take it easy, Bob!

A UNIFORMED COP calls out.

                    COP
         Hey, Baxter! It's Commissioner Garrett.

The COP points to a sedan. Behind the wheel sits POLICE COMMISSIONER
GARRETT, a small, severe, crewcut man of sixty five.

BAXTER hurries over.

JACK handcuffs the THIRD SUSPECT and leads all three towards a police car.

Another police car releases BARKING DOGS.

JACK glances at BAXTER and the COMMISSIONER. They are arguing. BAXTER
slams his hand down on the sedan hood.

A German Shepherd jumps up on JACK, both paws on his chest as she tries to lick
his face. JACK pushes the dog back.

                    JACK
         For Christ's sake, Lorenzo, can't you control
         your damn dog?

                    DOG HANDLER
         She's sweet on you, Jack. It's your animal
         magnetism.

The COMMISSIONER drives away.

BAXTER comes over.

                    JACK
         What did Garrett want?

                    BAXTER
         Nothing much. The usual bullshit.
         You want to grab a beer?

                    JACK
         Not tonight.

                    BAXTER
         Come on. I'll buy you a cold one. There's
         something I want to talk to you about.

                    JACK
          Tell me tomorrow, buddy.
          I'm headed for a warm bath.

JACK heads for a patrol car.

                    BAXTER
            Jack, hold on –

BAXTER is surrounded by barking dogs.

JACK waves, gets in the car.

JACK'S PLACE   EXT   NIGHT

JACK's two room adobe house is jammed up against a tall mesh fence.
On the far side are the landing lights of Davis Monthan Air Force Base.

JACK works beneath a corrugated plastic roof on the motor of his TR-7.
He wears a clean white shirt. His hands are covered with oil but the rest
of his workshop is spotless.

Spread out by an empty corral is JACK's collection of non-functional vehicles.

The sound of crickets.

HEADLIGHTS APPEAR.

JACK carefully wipes his hands on a rag and walks slowly to the dirt driveway.

BAXTER pulls up in an unmarked police car.

                    JACK
            Hi, Bob. Want a soda?

JACK'S PLACE   INT   NIGHT

JACK and BAXTER are seated in JACK's spartan living room.

On the coffee table are three radios in various states of repair, a broken-down
clock, a tool kit, a soldering iron and a cup of cold tea.

On the formica mantelpiece sit a rodeo trophy, a picture of JACK's sixteen year
old daughter, and a Chinese hand grenade. A hand-lettered sign reads:
NOT A TOY! In English and Chinese.

                    JACK
          You're fuckin' insane, Bob.

                    BAXTER
          You're right, Jack. I'm nuts. I'm in the
          worst trouble I've ever been in. And I'm
          asking you to help me. I won't blame you
          if you say no.

                    JACK
          You're asking me to help you commit
          a murder.

                    BAXTER
          Quintana is class A scum, Jack. He's a
          drug-dealing degenerate. He doesn't
          deserve to be alive.

In the distance – a train whistle.

                    JACK
          You don't know what you're saying, Bob.
          Best thing for you to do is tell the truth
          and take your chances.

                    BAXTER
          Don't give me that righteous bullshit!
          Damn it! I'm your friend, Jack. We've
          been partners for ten years and I never
          asked you for a damn thing.

He stares bitterly at his soda bottle while JACK drinks slowly from his can of beer.

                    BAXTER
          I'm in over my head. If I don't smoke
          Quintana I'm a dead man.

                    JACK
          Why? Who owns you, Bob?

BAXTER shakes his head.

                    BAXTER
          I can't tell you. Yes or no, Jack?
          It's coming down in twenty minutes.

                    JACK
          No.

BAXTER stands up.

                    BAXTER
          Fuck you.

Through the window, JACK watches BAXTER walk towards his car.

As BAXTER drives away, JACK goes over to the chest of drawers
where his pistol and holster lie.

He checks the cylinder of his .45 Peacemaker.

TR-7   INT   NIGHT

JACK sits behind the wheel of his English sports car.

Traffic is pulled up ahead of him while a giant bulldozer reverses across the road.

DOWNTOWN TUCSON   EXT   NIGHT

The TR-7 screams around a corner. Ahead is the Amtrak depot.

GUNSHOTS are heard.

TRACKS   EXT   NIGHT

JACK jumps out, gun in hand.

A LIMO squeals around the corner, knocking down a street sign.
It disappears into the underpass. One window is shot out.

BAXTER and another MAN lie dead on the railroad tracks.

A third MAN, well dressed, distinguished – QUINTANA – walks slowly away,
across the tracks. He has been shot several times.

JACK runs after him.

                    JACK
          Police Officer! FREEZE!

QUINTANA keeps on walking. In one hand, he clutches a briefcase.
In the other, he holds a gun.

JACK levels his pistol at QUINTANA.

                         JACK
                  Drop the weapon! Now!

QUINTANA turns and looks at JACK. He tries to speak but blood gurgles in his
throat.

JACK stares at him. QUINTANA's eyes drift past JACK to something above him.

                        QUINTANA
                  Pinche cabron...

He drops the gun and falls to his knees.

JACK turns. Looks up.

ANGLE ON A HUGE BILLBOARD

advertising a sanitarium and rehab clinic. Its white-haired, white-clad proprietor
beams down. A MAN crouches on the catwalk in front of the sign, aiming a RIFLE.

JACK dives for cover behind BAXTER's car.

A bullet hits the pavement. No sound from the silenced gun.

ANGLE ON QUINTANA

Pitching forward on his face. The briefcase hits a rail, and breaks open.
It is full of money.

Money blows everywhere.

JACK hears footsteps on a metal ladder. He peers over the hood –

Another bullet breaks the windshield.

JACK retreats beneath the car.

Another bullet slams into the front tire.

The car slowly lowers.

POLICE SIRENS.

JACK crawls out to face armed COPS.

TUCSON CITY SKYLINE   EXT   DAY

MONTAGE of RADIO and TV VOICES.

                    RADIO VOICE
          Strong rumors persist that a vigilante
          group is operating in the Tucson area –

                    TV VOICE
          – the so-called Death Squad, which is alleged
          to include police officers, was apparently
          involved in the murder of a prominent
          Sonoran businessman, Charles Quintana.

                    RADIO VOICE
          -- named tonight as leaders of the renegades
          were Department of Public Safety officers
          Robert Baxter and Jack Ditko. Baxter was
          recently slain in a shoot-out at the Amtrak
          Station –

                    TV VOICE
          -- and Detective Ditko has been relegated
          to the Tactical Support Division pending a
          full investigation.

TUCSON POLICE DEPT   INT   DAY

JACK and RICHARDSON stare at a video monitor.

JACK is clean and shaved.

ON THE MONITOR

We see a body lying beneath a sheet. Beside it stands the CORONER.

HIGH ANGLE, as from a surveillance camera.

A MAN and a WOMAN enter. The WOMAN is tall, stunningly attractive
and well dressed: ANGELA. The MAN is shorter than she, extremely muscular,
wearing a World Gym shirt: FLOYD.

                    RICHARDSON
          Not bad, huh?

                    JACK
          Who is she?

                    RICHARDSON
          Quintana's wife.

The CORONER pulls back the white sheet, revealing QUINTANA's corpse.

ANGELA QUINTANA's face shows no expression.

                    ANGELA
          That's him.

                    CORONER
          The money's being held as evidence but you
          can pick up his other belongings tomorrow.

                    ANGELA
          Keep them.

RICHARDSON freezes ANGELA's video image.

                    JACK
          RUN IT AGAIN.

RICHARDSON rewinds the video tape. Runs it again.
He hands JACK ANGELA's sheet.

                    RICHARDSON
          Quintana's old lady is a Mafia Princess.
          She was married to that limey mobster
          Bellville for six weeks. After he got smoked
          she took up with Quintana. Lived with him
          in Mexico for eight years. No children.

He zooms in on ANGELA's face.

                    JACK
               (reading the sheet)
          Eyes: one green, one gray.

Behind them, the door opens.

COMMISSIONER GARRETT appears. He motions to JACK.

<u>GARRETT'S OFFICE</u>   INT   DAY

JACK sits before the COMMISSIONER in his wood paneled Western-style office.
Reproductions of Remingtons. Cowhide couch. Polished oak desk.

Framed portraits of PRESIDENT REAGAN, the GOVERNOR, and the MAYOR.

The COMMISSIONER holds a document in each hand. One of 200 pages,
stamped with the City Seal. The other a three-page Incident Report.

                    GARRETT
          Jack, please. Listen to reason. This is
          the most thoroughly investigated incident
          in the history of the Department. We have
          reports from one hundred and twenty officers
          and witnesses, as well as the Coroner.
          They all say that Baxter died in an exchange
          of gunfire with Chalo Quintana.

                    JACK
          There weren't any witnesses.
          I was the first man on the scene.
          I was shot at by a man with a rifle.

GARRETT sighs, shaking his head.

                    GARRETT
          Jack, Jack... What do you want? A vacation?
          More time off? Want to come inside for a while?

JACK turns his straw hat in his hand.

                    JACK
          Nothing like that.

He gets up, heading for the door.

                    GARRETT
          If you don't get in line, you're going to cause
          a lot of problems. You have many friends here,
          Jack – friends you should stick up for.

JACK shakes his head, not knowing what to say.
He puts his hand on the doorknob.

GARRETT waves another paper.

                    GARRETT
          Sign this before you leave, Jack.
          Or don't bother coming back.

JACK pauses, ramrod straight, not looking left or right.
Then he goes out the door.

                    GARRETT V/O
          You are suspended from the Department
          for an indefinite period.

TR-7   INT   DAY

JACK drives away from downtown.

A SIREN behind.

He pulls over.

HIGHWAY   EXT   DAY

Two young COPS check every inch of the TR-7, looking for an infraction. There is none.

JACK sits behind the wheel.

JACK'S PLACE   EXT   DUSK

JACK stands in the arroyo behind his house, a stop watch in hand, practicing his quick draw.

In the arroyo front of him, a tire hangs.

After drawing and holstering several times, he fires off a shot.

The tire spins.

Inside the house, the phone rings.

JACK ignores the phone.

JACK'S PLACE   EXT   DAY

JACK sits outside his adobe in the hot sun.

ANGLE ON JACK'S FOOT

A large diamondback rattlesnake crawls past.

JACK hisses at the snake.

                    JACK
          Psssssss...

The snake slides away.

A MILITARY JET screams, coming in to land.

GRAYHOUND TRACK   EXT   NIGHT

BOB BAXTER's widow, VIOLET, and her sister, DOT, sit in the stand watching
the race. They pass a pint of Seagrams back and forth, pouring it into their
big-gulp ups of 7-Up.

JACK squeezes towards them.

                    JACK
          Hello, Violet.

VIOLET and DOT scream as the dogs head for the finish line.

                    VIOLET
          I didn't know you like dogs, Jack.

                    JACK
          I don't. I just wanted to come over and
          say I was sorry about Bob.
               (he pauses, uncertain)
          He was a damned good man.

                    VIOLET
          Bullshit. He was a lousy cop and a lousy
          husband. Violent and crazy. We should
          have split up a long time ago.

                    JACK
          Why didn't you?

                    VIOLET
          He got his own place a year ago.
          I didn't see much of him.

                    JACK
          Bob has his own place?

VIOLET and DOT scream as another race begins.

                    JACK
          Where was Bob's place?

                    VIOLET
          Down on Speedway by the second
          Circle K, past the University.

                    JACK
          What is it, an apartment?

                    VIOLET
          A condo. In one of those new buildings
          down there.

JACK is surprised.

                    JACK
          Those places are over two hundred grand.
          Do you have a key?

                    VIOLET
          Getting one tomorrow. I'm going to get rid
          of his shit and put it on the market.

                    DOT
          Shit!

VIOLET and DOT tear up their tickets.

A BIG MAN in a Panama Hat – MULLER – barges up. He is very drunk.

                    MULLER
          Say, you're Jock, what's his name, Dildo,
          aren't you? The cop who wouldn't sign
          that cover-up report?

A professional look comes over JACK's face – cold and non-commital.
He steps back, out of reach.

                    JACK
               (quiet, polite)
          No. You've got the wrong fellow.

                    MULLER
          No, come on, open up! I'm Phil Muller from
          the Star. I covered that whole story. You're
          the guy. You blew away that Mexican Mafia
          don at the station – I was on that train!

                    JACK
          You have me confused with someone else.

                    MULLER
          Now, wait just a minute...

He grabs hold of JACK's arm. JACK is extremely tense.

VIOLET pulls a silver-plated .38 out of her purse.

                    VIOLET
          Listen to me, you. I just got done burying
          my husband and feel intimidated by your
          aggressive posture. Back the fuck off or
          I'll shoot you in the fucking balls.

The wind goes out of MULLER's sails. He goes away.

                    VIOLET
          Hate to see a cop get ragged, no matter
          how fucked up he is.

                    JACK
          Call me tomorrow when you get the key.

                    VIOLET
          What key?

                    JACK
          The key to Bob's place. I'll go over with you.

She turns her attention to the next race.

JACK walks away.

PARKING LOT   EXT   NIGHT

JACK heads for his TR-7. Behind him, the roar of the track.

He unlocks the driver's door, removes the steering wheel anti-theft lock.

Thunder and heat lightning.

BOB BAXTER'S CONDO   INT   DAY

VIOLET and DOT open the door. JACK follows them inside.

A big, five-room layout, spare and expensive.

A high-tech gym in one room; another room with a king sized bed and giant, square box, TV with scattered VHS collection. The balcony overlooks another condo.

The living room is full of papers, some half-burned, ashes scattered near file cabinets and an open safe.

JACK looks through the burned stuff while VIOLET and DOT open a wall of enormous closet doors.

                    VIOLET
          Look at this creepy stuff. Who the
          fuck was he trying to impress?

Polyester cowboy shirts, elastic-waisted Levis fly into the center of the room.

                     DOT
             (opening the fridge)
          Vodka and cheese whiz! Let's have
          a picnic!

JACK studies the half-burned envelopes and receipts.

Figures and dates have been obliterated, but the envelopes carry the return
address of the Regency Clinic.

CLOSE ON

Another return address: REGENCY CLINIC, CR. NED MOUNT, PHD, DRS, PSI.

                    JACK
          You've got a lovely place here, Violet.

VIOLET looks up from the floor where she and DOT are sifting through a box
of belt buckles and turquoise jewelry, drinking vodka and eating processed cheese.
She smiles at JACK.

                    VIOLET
          You want to christen it with us?

JACK tips his hat to them.

                    JACK
          Maybe some other time.

He leaves.

<u>REGENCY HEALTH CENTER</u>   EXT   DAY

A secluded, rambling TREATMENT CENTER against a magnificent mountain
backdrop. Adjacent is a golf course.

(It is same resort seen on the billboard with the picture of the white-haired MAN)

JACK drives up in his TR-7.

A white limo with California plates pulls out of the main gate.
It passes JACK, heading west.

CENTER PARKING LOT   EXT   DAY

JACK mops his brow, walks across the shimmering lawn to the CENTER –

-- a cheerful, hotel-style complex set in the foothills of the Tucson Mountains. Half a mile away, higher in the foothills, sits a windowless adobe structure with solar panels on the roof.

A narrow road winds up to it.

REGENCY CENTER RECEPTION   INT   DAY

Southwestern décor with huge windows that overlook a mountain panorama. There are more maids and porters than hospital staff.

Discreet signs indicate IN-PATIENTS, OUT-PATIENTS, SECLUSION WARDS, PHARMACY, SAUNA, TANNING SALON...

JACK mingles with a group of newly-arrived IN-PATIENTS.

They are being oriented by a kindly physician in her 60s, DR. RUTH BENWAY.

                    DR. BENWAY
          Naturally, we at Regency Health hope
          that your stays will all be brief, and
          pleasant, but most of all we hope that
          they will be organic. Remember, every
          fresh breath we take, every habit we
          dispose of, every pound we shed, is a
          sliver dollar in the bank of health!

The GROUP knows they've come to the right place.

INTERNS usher the IN-PATIENTS towards waiting golf karts.

JACK walks up to the reception desk.

                    JACK
               (to RECEPTIONIST)
          Dr. Ned Mount, please.

                    RECEPTIONIST
          Do you have an appointment?

                    JACK
          I don't. But I think he'll see me.
          I was Bob Baxter's partner.

The RECEPTIONIST checks out a name in her computer. JACK looks around.

> RECEPTIONIST
> Dr. Mount, please... Yes, Doctor, this is
> Reception. There's a gentleman here to
> see you. He was a friend of Bob Baxter.

Through the big plate-glass window, JACK's eye falls on a patch of desert
spotted with giant Saguaro cactus immediately below the windowless
white adobe.

ANGLE ON TWO CHILDREN

Running in and out of the arroyo. A MAN in a white orderly's coat runs after them.

ANGLE ON JACK

The RECEPTIONIST smiles at him. He smiles back.

> RECEPTIONIST
> I'm real sorry, sir. Dr. Mount is busy
> right at the moment. If you'd like to wait
> awhile there's some herbal tea and
> carrot juice across the lobby.

JACK follows her pointed finger.

ANGLE ON A VENERABLE MOVIE STAR

Coming through, followed by white-coated attendants, a personal assistant, etc.

An OLD MAN in the Regency's black kimono-bathrobe approaches, holding a paper
for the CELEBRITY to sign.

The CELEBRITY and RETINUE sail out through the main door towards a pair
of waiting limos.

Holding open the door is a short, extremely muscular young man wearing a
tight leather jacket and green paisley pants.

Something about him jars JACK's memory.

> RECEPTIONIST
> Don't you just love that show?
> Of all the re-runs it's my favorite.

JACK continues to stare at the MAN. FLASH:

The VIDEO SCREEN showing ANGELA QUINTANA and her companion – FLOYD.

                    RECEPTIONIST
          Who else was in it? That big guy with the
          white hat. The one whose shirts were
          always too short for him?

                    JACK
          That was Bonanza.

ANGLE ON JACK

Watching as FLOYD circles the lobby, looks around, goes out again.

JACK follows him.

PARKING LOT   EXT   DAY

FLOYD is standing on the hood of a black Trans Am, scanning the golf course
with binoculars.

Shaking his head, JACK observes discreetly from the main door.

FLOYD jumps down from the hood and gets into the Trans Am.

He peels out, burning rubber.

HIGHWAY   EXT   DAY

JACK's TR-7 follows the Trans Am towards the three tall buildings of downtown.

RENAISSANCE INN   EXT   DAY

JACK watches from the TR-7 as FLOYD takes a path between the pool-side condos.

FLOYD stops outside the door to APT. 63. He takes out a key and opens it,
goes inside, shutting the door behind him.

JACK exits his car and walks to APT. 63.

The blinds are drawn. Voices are heard within.

JACK leans up against the window. He sees the dim shapes of TWO MEN and a
WOMAN.

                    MAN'S VOICE
          He's playing golf? We'll take him on the
          ninth hole.

JACK'S POV

The shape of an AR-15 rifle with a SNIPER'S SCOPE, sliding into a golf bag.

> FLOYD'S VOICE
> (muffled)
> What about the money?

The voice from the autopsy tape – ANGELA's – is heard.

> ANGELA'S VOICE
> When the job is done.

> FLOYD'S VOICE
> Fifty percent up front is what we said.

> MAN'S VOICE
> Afraid?

A sudden movement behind the blind.

The sound of a hand SLAPPING a cheek.

> ANGELA'S VOICE
> Stop fighting! We're wasting time!

Immediately TWO SHAPES head for the door.

JACK steps back sharply, knocks on the door of APT. 64.

FLOYD emerges, shrugging into a jacket, a .38 in a holster on his belt. JACK concentrates on the door in front of him. It opens.

An elderly WOMAN with an I'M WITH STUPID tee shirt looks at him.

> WOMAN
> Hi!

> JACK
> I'm looking for Mr. DeSoto.

JACK glances back as FLOYD and a straight-backed, gray-haired Latino – O'BRIEN - walk towards the Trans Am. O'BRIEN carries the golf bag.

> WOMAN
> DeSoto? ... Well, let me just think.
> Milton – what was that couple's name
> we met in the Sundowner Lounge?

ANGLE ON ANGELA QUINTANA

Standing in the doorway. She wears a white silk cowboy shirt, tight French jeans tucked into multi-colored alligator boots. A sultry knockout and definitely all business, ANGELA is at the top of her game.

The WOMAN's HUSBAND appars, wearing a tee shirt that says, STUPID.

                    HUSBAND
          I think their name was Nince.
          You're welcome to use our phone to
          call the front desk.

ANGELA turns, looks for a moment toward JACK.
She has one gray eye and one green eye.

JACK steps up to her, tipping his straw hat.

                    JACK
          Angela! Angela Quintana!

ANGELA freezes, not knowing what to expect.

                    WOMAN
          (eyeing ANGELA)
          Well, I guess he found what he was
          looking for.

                    HUSBAND
          (laughing, to JACK)
          Have a good one, pardner!

                    JACK
          You and I met down in Acapulco, damn it,
          it must be six or seven years ago.

She turns her back on him, to go inside.

                    ANGELA
          If you'll excuse me.

                    JACK
          Sorry about your husband. They set him
          up, of course.

APT. 63   INT DAY

JACK is inside, shutting the door before she can react.

He scans the room with a professional eye.

                    ANGELA
               (impatiently)
          Who are you?

                    JACK
          Nince. Milton Nince. An old friend of Chalo's.
          Business partner, you might say.

She opens the door.

                    ANGELA
          I'm not interested in your business, Mr., ah,
          Nince. If you don't mind, I have a headache
          and am very tired.

                    JACK
          Of course. I understand.
          May I use your bathroom?

JACK strides across the room to the bathroom.

BATHROOM   INT   DAY

He locks the door.

Taking a leak, he lifts the top off the toilet. Sure enough, there's a big black
AUTOMATIC in a plastic bag.

JACK looks in the medicine cabinet. It is empty.

He unlocks the door.

APT. 63   INT   DAY

ANGELA sits on the couch, crying.

JACK sits down into a chair opposite her, shaking his head.

He picks up some envelopes from the coffee table, looks them over.
Glances at the labels on her luggage, packed and ready to go.

                    JACK
          Staying long?

She sobs more bitterly.

JACK absently turns on the TV with a remote control.

                    JACK
          These guys you have working for you,
          Ms. Quintana. They're not good enough.

                    ANGELA
          I know. You're right. All they do is
          cause me stress.

                    JACK
          Your husband promised me a job.

                    ANGELA
          Fuck you. I don't have time to deal with
          your problems.

                    JACK
          My problems could be the solution to your
          problems. Chalo and I, we go way back.

                    ANGELA
          My husband didn't associate with dipsticks
          and low rent hoods. Mister, get lost.

JACK rises, goes to the door.

                    JACK
          If you change your mind, I'm staying at the
          Americana. I think you can use some help.

Their eyes cross as JACK goes out.

ANGELA locks the door.

She looks at the TV: *Throne of Blood.*

HIGHWAY   EXT   DAY

JACK speeds along the highway.

He turns into the Country Club adjacent to the Regency Health Center.

COUNTRY CLUB   EXT   DAY

The TR-7 pulls up next to the Trans Am. JACK sees FLOYD and O'BRIEN
get into a golf kart and speed away.

JACK looks for another kart. The KART MARSHAL approaches.

> KART MARSHAL
> Excuse me, sir! Excuse me! May I help you?

> JACK
> I need one of these karts. As quick as you can.

> KART MARSHAL
> I'm sorry, sir. This is a private club.

> JACK
> I know that. But I have a meeting.

> KART MARSHAL
> You'll have to go to the Club House and
> register as a house guest, if, of course,
> you have a sponsor.

JACK takes off, running.

GOLF COURSE   EXT   DAY

JACK pants up to the second hole. He's sweating profusely in the 100 degree heat.

He sees FLOYD's kart disappear over a rise.

He runs toward two elderly WOMEN sitting in a kart.

They speed off as JACK approaches.

ANOTHER PART OF THE GOLF COURSE   EXT   DAY

JACK, winded and clutching his side, reaches the fourth hole.

He is pursued by the KART MARSHAL in his official kart.

No sign of FLOYD or O'BRIEN.

JACK sees a virile, white-haired man – COLONEL WOODROW AMES, the benign
doctor from the billboard – and his party standing between two parked karts.

He also sees the glint of a RIFLE in a patch of carefully curated cactus.

JACK runs, shouting and waving, towards COLONEL AMES, who is bent
over his putter.

                    JACK
                GET DOWN!

The COLONEL'S PARTY turns and stares. One of the golfers is POLICE
COMMISSIONER GARRETT. Another is a large, swarthy BUSINESS
ASSOCIATE with bi-focals.

AMES concentrates on his putt.

An AIDE pulls out a GUN.

                    GARRETT
                What the hell! Ditko!

                    JACK
                Into the sand trap!

Everyone looks at the sand trap and back at JACK.

VIA SNIPER SIGHTS

We see the COLONEL in the cross-hairs.

ANGLE ON THE COLONEL

His concentration breaks. Impatiently, he rises –

BANG!

The BUSINESS ASSOCIATE is shot in the head.

Everyone scrambles for the sand trap.

The AIDE shoots at JACK.

MORE GUNFIRE from the cactus patch.

                    AMES
                Not him! Over there! The cactus!

The AIDE fires at the cactus patch.

JACK drags the COLONEL towards the sand trap.

BANG! BANG!

The KART MARSHAL falls from his kart, shot in the foot.

His kart careens away.

<u>SAND TRAP</u>   EXT   DAY

JACK drags COLONEL AMES to safety, helped by the AIDE.

JACK is exhausted. COMMISSIONER GARRETT is enraged.

> GARRETT
> Ditko, you have no authority!

> JACK
> Keep your head down.
> (to AIDE)
> Two males with rifles on the hill above
> the fourth hole. One Caucasian, 25.
> One dark complexioned, 45 or 50.

GARRETT crawls over to the AIDE and grabs his walkie talkie.

COLONEL AMES studies JACK intently.

> AMES
> Who are you?

> JACK
> Name's Jack Ditko, sir. Do you know
> the deceased?

> AMES
> A business associate. You're not
> Billy Ray Ditko's boy, are you?

> JACK
> Yes, sir, I am.

> AMES
> They don't make 'em like your old man
> any more. Best damn bronc buster in
> the State of Arizona. Is he still alive?

> JACK
> Yes, sir, he is. Keep your head down.

BANG! BANG!

Bullets splatter the lip of the sand trap above them.

> JACK
> Any idea who's out there?

                    AMES
          Nope. I don't know of any men who have
          this sort of aversion towards me.
          A few women, of course.

                    JACK
          What about your business associate?

                    AMES
          Mustafa just got here from Turkey. This
          is his first visit. I can't imagine...

                 1st BUSINESSMAN
          Must be a kidnapping attempt.

                 2nd BUSINESSMAN
            I hope to God it's not political!
Above, the sound of HELICOPTERS.

APPROACHING SIRENS.

<u>REGENCY CENTER</u>   EXT   AFTERNOON

An ambulance pulls into the parking lot, followed by JACK and GARRETT
in a golf kart. JACK drives.

                    GARRETT
          There's more to this than meets the eye,
          Ditko. They way I see it the towel heads
          are behind it. They hate the guys who dress
          like westerners. Entrepreneurs. That's a
          whole despised class, you know. Makes
          'em crazy. They become terrorists.
          Know what the worst of it is?

                    DITKO
          What, Commissioner?

                    GARRETT
          The State is filling up with them.
          More and more every day.

COLONEL AMES helped from the ambulance. He strides forward,
shaking off the MEDIC. He's instantly enveloped by his entourage.

ANGLE ON A GIRL

- running up to him – RUBY. A stunning raven-haired beauty of nineteen;
Mestiza or Indian.

                         RUBY
              What happened, Woodrow?

                         AMES
              Mr. Mustapha got shot.

                         RUBY
              Fatally?

                         AMES
              I'm afraid so.

                         RUBY
              Who did it?

                         AMES
              Psychos. Probably Turks.
              Political extremists.

He gestures towards JACK.

                         AMES
              This young fella saved the day.
              Billy Ray Ditko's boy, Jake.

                         JACK
              Jack.

                         RUBY
              Billy Ray Ditko who won the State steer
              roping contest seven years in a row?

                         JACK
                    (diffident)
              That's him. You have a good memory.

                         RUBY
              I do. I'm Ruby.

COLONEL AMES motions to another trendy, GQ AIDE in an elegant linen
cowboy suit.

                         AMES
              Jack, I'd like you to meet one of my top
              aides, Dr. Ned Mount.

DR. NED MOUNT absently shakes JACK's hand.

ANGLE ON RANDY

Large and beefy, with a listening device in his ear, joining them.

> AMES
> And this is Randy, my Chief of Security,
> charged with my personal safety at
> all times –

RANDY whispers in the COLONEL's ear. The COLONEL looks displeased.

> AMES
> (sotto voce)
> Only one? But there were two of 'em.

The COLONEL and his GROUP move on. JACK and DR. NED are left behind.

> DR. NED
> Anarchy. Those Turks are tough, and
> ruthless. They have one of the top
> three foreign legions in the world.

ANGLE ON MUSTAFA'S CORPSE

Being wheeled aboard an ambulance.

> JACK
> Doctor Ned Mount. Right?

> DR. NED
> Yes. Please excuse me.

> JACK
> I'm Jack Ditko, Bob Baxter's partner.

> DR. NED
> Damn shame about Bob. He was doing so
> well. He'd been clean for over a year.

> JACK
> Didn't he work here?

> DR. NED
> No. Why do you mean? He was my
> patient in rehab.

                    JACK
          I could have sworn he told me he was
          on the payroll.

                    DR. NED
          Excuse me, Mr., ah, eh. Sorry again
          about your partner.

DR. NED MOUNT heads briskly for the Clinic.

TR-7   INT   EVENING

JACK drives away from the Center, past the Golf Course.

HIS POV:

The body of FLOYD is put into the back of another ambulance by two PRIVATE
SECURITY MEN. FLOYD has a bullet hole in his forehead.

A MOTORCYCLE COP waves JACK's car by.

APT. 63   INT   NIGHT

JACK picks the lock and enters.

The phone rings. JACK picks it up. A hang-up.

He looks around. The room is empty.

The TV is still on, white noise emerging from it.

There is a pile of ashes in the ashtray and on the coffee table.

JACK goes to the kitchenette, takes Saran Wrap from a drawer,
and Saranwraps the coffee table.

A KNOCK ON THE DOOR.

JACK steps into the hall closet.

RANDY and a SECURITY MAN enter. Both carry guns.

                    RANDY
          Angela?

JACK, in the closet, holds the door slightly ajar with his left hand.
His pistol is in his right.

ANGLE ON RANDY AND SECURITY MAN

Checking out the empty suite.

                    SECURITY MAN
          They wrapped the coffee table.

                    RANDY
          Cops.

He kicks over the coffee table as they leave.

PARKING LOT   EXT   NIGHT

JACK carries the broken coffee table to his car.

HIGHWAY   EXT   NIGHT

The coffee table, too large to fit inside the TR-7, is bunjy-corded to the roof.
JACK drives out of town. SIRENS in the distance.

JACK'S PLACE   INT   NIGHT

JACK sits with the new coffee table placed on top of the old one.

All the living room lights are focused on the work at hand – his painstaking
reconstruction of the burned material.

The phone rings. He picks it up.

                    JACK
          Ditko.

                    RUBY'S VOICE
          Mr. Ditko. This is Ruby. You met me
          at the Center.

                    JACK
          I remember.

                    RUBY'S VOICE
          What are you doing tomorrow afternoon?

                    JACK
          Depends.

REGENCY CENTER   EXT   NIGHT

RUBY walks back and forth on a spacious balcony, talking on a cordless phone.

Below her, on the patio, in various states of relaxation, are PATIENTS,
all wearing black silk kimonos.

>   RUBY
> Say around three or three fifteen?
> The Colonel's making an Environmental
> Impact Statement out at the old San
> Xavier Mine. You know the spot?

>   JACK'S VOICE
> I do.

>   RUBY
> So come on out! You can see Woodrow,
> I mean, the Colonel. He know your partner,
> so you'll have plenty to discuss.

ANGLE ON DR. NED MOUNT

Seated at a glass table with RANDY, looking aghast.

>   JACK'S VOICE
> Okay, then, Ms. Ruby. Do you have a
> last name?

>   RUBY
> Diamante.

She turns the phone off and throws it to DR. NED MOUNT.

In the background, a Kitt Peak Astronomer lectures on the stars,
and Asian music plays.

>   DR. NED
> Well, is he coming?

>   RUBY
> What do you think?

She walks away. RANDY laughs.

>   RANDY
> For her, he comes.
> For you, forget it.

<u>JACK'S PLACE</u>   INT   NIGHT

CLOSE ON TWEEZERS

Lifting the last fragment of a match book.

Nothing is revealed.

The phone rings.

> JACK
> (picking it up)
> Hello.

> ANGELA'S VOICE
> Jack? Jack Ditko? This is Angela Quintana.

A long pause.

> JACK
> Yes?

> ANGELA'S VOICE
> We need to talk. I knew your partner.
> Meet me in Douglas at the Cortez Hotel.

> JACK
> What time?

> ANGELA'S VOICE
> Any time.

<u>TR-7</u>   INT   NIGHT

JACK drives towards the border. A sign says: MEXICO 50 KILOMETERS.

<u>CORTEZ HOTEL, DOUGLAS</u>   EXT   DAWN

The TR-7 pulls up outside the hotel – a decaying colonial structure near the railroad tracks.

JACK gets out. He goes into the hotel.

ANGLE ON A FORD LTD

ANGELA gets out of the passenger seat and follows JACK into the hotel.

O'BRIEN – the dapper gray-haired Mexican, sporting a pencil moustache - sits in the driver's seat.

CORTEZ HOTEL LOBBY   INT   DAWN

JACK is at the front desk of the huge ornate lobby, decorated with pillars and stained glass windows.

> JACK
> (to CLERK)
> Angela Quintana.

The CLERK looks over JACK's shoulder, to the door.

JACK turns. ANGELA comes towards him.

> ANGELA
> You're up early, Mr. Ditko. It is Ditko,
> isn't it? Or is it Nince?

> JACK
> Ditko. Any place to eat around here?

> ANGELA
> No place good. Let's go to my room.

They walk up the stairs.

ANGELA'S ROOM   INT   DAY

ANGELA stands by the window.

JACK is seated in a low cane chair by the bed.

> ANGELA
> So what do you want to do, Mr. Ditko?
> Get even?

> JACK
> With who?

> ANGELA
> With the man who killed my husband
> and your partner.

> JACK
> And who might that be?

ANGELA looks at him for a long moment – wary, mocking, dangerous.

>   ANGELA
> You haven't figured it out, have you?

>   JACK
> Not all of it.

>   ANGELA
> Not any of it. Your partner and my husband
> were killed by Colonel Ames. He had them
> blown away, at the railroad station.

>   JACK
> Why?

>   ANGELA
> Because Baxter was too greedy, and Chalo
> wanted out.

>   JACK
> I don't believe you.

>   ANGELA
> You're really an asshole. I bet you shoot at
> tires in your back yard. You've got a 30.30
> and a pickup. Am I right?

>   JACK
>   (impatient, off-guard)
> Your husband was a drug-dealing scum.
> You don't know the half of it.

>   ANGELA
> Wrong, wrong, wrong. He wasn't a drug
> dealer. He was a body dealer. Just like
> your partner, Bob.

JACK doesn't get it. He stands up, then sits down again.

>   JACK
> Are you saying that Bob was ...

ANGELA pulls open a drawer. Takes a shot of tequila and hands JACK the bottle.

>   ANGELA
> Let's go for a walk.

<u>INTERNATIONAL STREET, DOUGLAS</u>   EXT   DAY

JACK and ANGELA walk along the fence that separates the American town of Douglas from the Mexican town of Agua Prieta, twenty feet away.

The bottle is half empty. JACK takes a sip, hands it to ANGELA.

>   ANGELA
> Chalo moved illegal immigrants.
> The Colonel had an interest in ...
> children. Baxter found out about it,
> and cut himself in.

An ALARM goes off in a nearby building.

JACK rubs his eyes.

>   JACK
> You mean an adoption ring?

>   ANGELA
> No.

>   JACK
> There's worse things than that.
> It gives a kid a good home. Three
> squares a day. A decent education.

>   ANGELA
> This wasn't an adoption ring.
> These kids were SOLD.

>   JACK
> That doesn't happen here.

>   ANGELA
> I have to use the bathroom. Let's go back.

They turn and head towards the hotel.

<u>BATHROOM</u>   INT   DAY

ANGELA opens the cistern of the toilet.

She removes her gun from its plastic bag and wraps it in a towel.

<u>HOTEL ROOM</u>   INT   DAY

ANGELA packs the towel in her suitcase, which is open on the bed.

JACK sits by the window, drinking the last of the tequila.

They are both drunk.

                    JACK
          What a fuckin' mess. I knew Bob for
          sixteen years. I knew he was an asshole
          but corrupt ... no way.

                    ANGELA
          I thought the same about the Colonel.
          He stayed with us in Mexico. At our place
          in Zihuatanejo. I went off with him.
          Chalo was furious. But it was love.
          What can you do? And you know what
          really pissed me off? When he killed Chalo
          he didn't even try to kill me. I mean,
          who does he think I am?

                    JACK
          You're lucky. Maybe you should just
          head south.

                    ANGELA
          Forget it. I'm getting even with that
          motherfucker. He killed my partner.

                    JACK
          My partner was corrupt.

                    ANGELA
          He was still your partner.

ANGLE ON JACK

In the window. Thinking.

Beyond him a few cars and a truck are lined up on the Mexican side.

                    JACK
          I've been a cop for sixteen years.
          All that time I always had this little
          daydream. You know what it was?
          Just goin' hell for leather for the border
          with all the money I had saved up and   [CONT.]

                         JACK [CONT.]
               maybe some that wasn't mine.
               And never comin' back.
                         (looks at the street)
               I've never been as close as I am now.

JACK'S POV:

The street which leads to the Border. The LTD is still parked outside the hotel.

ANGELA walks over to him. She puts her arms around his neck. Leans in.

                         ANGELA
               We're in this together, Jack.
               Like it or not.

They kiss. A long beat.

                         ANGELA
               And I like it.

She turns away, shrugging out of her blouse.

JACK heads for the door, knocking over the tequila bottle.

ANGELA turns around. Her shirt is off.

They are both really drunk.

                         ANGELA
               Are you afraid?

JACK looks at her.

                         JACK
               Maybe. But I'm not stupid.

                         ANGELA
               That's funny. I had it the other way around.

HOTEL LOBBY   INT   DAY

JACK weaves through the lobby.

No one is around except for the DESK CLERK and the dapper O'BRIEN.

As JACK walks out the door, O'BRIEN follows him.

<u>STREET</u>   EXT DAY

JACK makes for his car.

O'BRIEN hurries up, waving a hotel bill.

> O'BRIEN
> Señor! Señor Rogers. Un momento,
> por favor. Your bill.

O'BRIEN looks appealingly at JACK.

> JACK
> You got the wrong hombre.

> O'BRIEN
> Oh, I am so sorry. You resemble so closely
> another cop, ah, customer ... a client of the
> hotel. You have a cigarette?

JACK starts looking for a cigarette, patting his pockets.
His pistol is exposed.

> JACK
> I forgot – I stopped smoking.

> O'BRIEN
> Why?

> JACK
> Not certain.

> O'BRIEN
> You Americans – you intend to live
> forever!

He smiles and opens the TR-7 door for JACK.

JACK drives away. Perplexed.

O'BRIEN watches him. Also perplexed.

He looks up at ANGELA's hotel window.

ANGLE ON ANGELA

Looking down. She shakes her head.

<u>DESERT</u> EXT DAY

Huge thunderclouds mass as JACK drives back towards Tucson.

<u>TR-7</u> INT DAY

JACK drives. His eyes are closing.

A few raindrops hit the windshield.

<u>SAN XAVIER MINE</u> EXT DAY

The TR-7 weaves through a sudden rainstorm along a narrow tarmac road.

On either side are endless white expanses of chemically treated mine tailings.

<u>MINE GATE</u> EXT DAY

The rain ends. The raindrops on JACK's windshield evaporate.

He gets out of the TR-7. Other cars and two local TV vans are parked nearby.

He walks towards a brightly colored awning set up near the rim of an
OPEN-PIT MINE.

A GREETER asks his name and pins a name tag on him.

A large banner reads: TUCSON ECO-VENTURE

It is very hot again, and windy. JACK sweats as he walks, white chemical dust
blowing around him in little eddies.

<u>ON THE RIM OF THE OPEN PIT</u> EXT DAY

Beneath the awning, a small group of REPORTERS and TV CAMERAS faces the
MAYOR of Tucson, various DIGNITARIES, and COLONEL AMES. The COLONEL
wears impenetrable shades.

The WARM WIND blows harder.

The COLONEL rises, to canned applause, and takes centre stage.

He speaks into the microphone.

                    AMES
          In 1980, NASA scientists came to me.
          They asked me if I could find a way to
          extend the human life process so that
          one man can live to travel to the stars –
          that's a journey of FIVE HUNDRED YEARS!

JACK walks closer, checking out the crowd.

On the far side of the little group, RANDY is doing the same.

The wind blows even harder.

                    AMES
          This voyage is possible. It is more than
          possible. It is our destiny.

Wild applause from the PA system.

                    AMES
          But, my friends, we are confronted with
          dark forces which seek to return science
          to the stone age. We must be vigilant against
          regressive, anti-science forces, whether
          they come wrapped in the garb of a priest,
          the denims of a radical environmentalist,
          or the striped tie and suit of a Washington
          bureaucrat.

The wind knocks down one of the awning poles.

Some of the empty seats are picked up and blown away.

                    AMES
          My friends, we WILL turn this corner,
          we WILL open this sacred door. We will
          enter together ... and sit down as one ...
          and play together the Great Symphony
          of Longevity, and Progress.

The CATERERS are running for their cars.

The CAMERA CREWS pack their equipment.

                    AMES
          Our Birthright. Our Fate.
          Our Promise to keep.

The applause dies as the pole-mounted speakers lose power.

Total confusion. Everyone flees the collapsing tent.

The awning flies away.

JACK walks up to AMES, unfazed by the chaotic scene.

> AMES
> How does FIVE HUNDRED YEARS sound
> to you, Ditko?

> JACK
> Boring.

The COLONEL laughs.

> AMES
> You are a character, sir. You say exactly
> what you feel, don't you? I admire that.

He takes JACK's arm. Watches as his SECURITY PERSONNEL run around
in shambles. Cars collide. RANDY shouts at DR. NED. Dust is everywhere.

> AMES
> Want to head up my Security Team?

> JACK
> (shouting above the wind)
> WHAT?

> AMES
> (shouting)
> You saved my life, Jack! I'm indebted
> to you! We'll start you at fifty grand -
> plus full medical and a new car every
> twelve months!

> JACK
> That won't be necessary.

> AMES
> (shouting)
> WHAT?

> JACK
> I'm sorry to say this, sir, but I'm going
> to see to it that you end up in jail.

COLONEL AMES seems shocked. He squeezes JACK's arm.

                    AMES
               Whatever for?

JACK shakes him off.

                    JACK
               Take your hand off me.

                    AMES
               Jack, I'm concerned about you. Don't go
               off and do something you might regret.

                    JACK
                    (straining to hear)
               WHAT? I have no regrets!

                    AMES
               Come up to the Center sometime soon,
               Jack, and we'll chat about it!

Neither man can see or hear the other.

WIDE SHOT

A giant TWISTER seeps along the rim of the open pit.

Everyone is lost in the DUST STORM.

TR-7   INT   DAY

Dust still blows.

JACK drives back to town on the two-lane blacktop.
He looks tired and confused, but also strangely elated.

Outside, a lightning flash, then thunder.

THROUGH THE WINDSHIELD

He sees a HUGE TRUCK coming directly at him.

JACK shouts!

TWO LANE BLACKTOP   EXT   DAY

JACK skids onto the soft shoulder, missing the TRUCK by inches.
The TR-7 spins out, slides into a newly-excavated road ditch.

<u>TWO LANE BLACKTOP</u>   EXT   DAY

JACK studies the TR-7. Both axles are broken. Oil is pouring from the pan.

He shakes his head.

Starts walking down the side of the road.

<u>DIRT ROAD</u>   EXT   DAY

Exhausted, JACK walks down a dirt road.

He opens a barbed wire gate with a metal sign: DITKO.

<u>BILLY RAY DITKO'S RANCH</u>   EXT   DAY

JACK approaches his father's ranch – two trailers set at right angles.

In back, a crude corral hosts three horses.

BILLY RAY pitches hay into the corral. He wears a straw hat and a faded cowboy shirt. He looks like an old rodeo cowboy, which is what he was.

BILLY RAY barely looks up as JACK stands beside hm.

                JACK
        How you doin', Pop?

                BILLY RAY
        Help yourself to a pitch fork, son.

It's boiling hot. JACK takes off his shirt.

                JACK
        I busted up my car.

JACK digs in with the pitch fork.

BILLY RAY watches him from the shade of the trailer.

                BILLY RAY
          (snorts)
        That little bitty English thing?
        I don't wonder. Those machines ain't
        built to be used. I hear you got fired.

                    JACK
Yeah.

                  BILLY RAY
You lasted longer than I thought you
would. I reckon it wasn't your fault.

                    JACK
Yeah. Say, Dad, you ever run into a
Colonel Ames?

                  BILLY RAY
Woodrow Ames? I know him.

                    JACK
What do you make of him?

                  BILLY RAY
Your mother and I had this spread down
on Big Creek. You remember it. Colonel
Ames comes ridin' up one day in three
brand-new jeeps. Him and a bunch from
back east. They made me an offer on the
place. Wanted to buy it up for some damn
fool nature preserve. I turned 'em down
flat. Run 'em off. Three nights later some
Mexican kid took a shot of me outside
El Minuto.

                    JACK
You're saying the Colonel was behind it?

                  BILLY RAY
Any damn fool would know that. So I
went up to that Clinic he's got. I walked
right into the damn operatin' theater.
He was standing there with a heart in
his hand and I told him that if he didn't
leave me and my land alone, I'd kill him.
I never heard from him again.

                    JACK
Pop, you really are loco. Those boys up
there are shrinks. Like at Betty Ford.
They ain't into cuttin' and stitchin'.

                  BILLY RAY
Suit yourself. I saw what I saw.

                    JACK
          Like the time you saw the flyin' disk
          over Gates Pass.

                    BILLY RAY
          Wasn't the only one. You know what's
          wrong with you? You're still thinkin'
          like a cop.
                    (takes off his straw hat,
                     taps his forehead)
          Brain dead.

JACK throws the pitch fork down.

                    BILLY RAY
          How about some coffee?

The old man turns and they both head for the trailers.

<u>JACK'S PLACE</u>   EXT   NIGHT

Cicadas chirp loudly as JACK puts a clean battery into his battered pickup truck.

He connects the battery. Gets in and turns the key. Nothing.
He gets back out and slides under the truck.

Suddenly the chirping of the cicadas STOPS.

JACK tenses, then rolls to the side between the truck and an empty oil drum.

MACHINE GUN FIRE!

Bullets rip through the drum.

JACK drops into the arroyo. Half crawling, he scrambles towards the house.

Bullets ricochet around him as he goes through the kitchen door.

<u>JACK'S PLACE</u>   INT   NIGHT

JACK slams the door shut.

Windows shatter.

From beneath his bed he pulls out his 30.30 and a box of cartridges.

Methodically, he loads the rifle.

He crawls to a broken window, waits for a break in the gunfire.

Standing, he fires one shot and ducks back down.

Outside, a MAN's voice yells and curses.

A motorcycle coughs and sputters, then roars off.

JACK waits.

JACK'S PLACE   INT   DAWN

JACK seeps behind the couch, the 30.30 in his lap.

He wakes. Standing up, he steps carefully through the broken glass and splintered wood.

The bathroom is shot to pieces.

He washes his face in the kitchen sink.

He looks out the window. A TPD unmarked car is parked by the corral.

JACK steps outside, shutting the door behind him.

JACK'S PLACE   EXT   DAWN

The sun is just coming up. JACK approaches the unmarked car.

Detectives RICHARDSON and ORTEGA sit inside, grinning at him over a fresh breakfast of coffee and Hole in the Wall donuts.

                    JACK
                 (pissed off)
          What are you guys doing?

                    ORTEGA
          Tailing you, Jack.

                    JACK
          What for?

                    ORTEGA
          Who knows? The Commissioner sent us.

ORTEGA and RICHARDSON get out. RICHARDSON offers him a donut.

                    RICHARDSON
          The word is that you're running around
          acting crazy. They say you got Post
          Traumatic Stress Syndrome on account
          of Bob.

                       JACK
          Bob was an asshole.

                      ORTEGA
          No doubt about that.

JACK walks towards his pickup. The DETECTIVES follow him.

                    RICHARDSON
          What's the matter with you, Jack?
          You're no longer on the case, man.
          You got to be –

He breaks off. They all stare at JACK's truck. The windows are shot out,
and there are bullet holes in the doors and hood.

                      ORTEGA
          You got a junk vehicle visible from the
          road. That's a hundred dollar fine.

                       JACK
          This isn't a junk vehicle.

He gets into the truck, and turns the key.

Amazingly, the pickup starts right up.

                       JACK
          I'll see you around.

He drives off.

RICHARDSON and ORGEGA pile into their unmarked car and peel after him,
bumping down the rutted dirt road. Their muffler is torn off.

JACK widens the distance between them.

<u>DESERT</u>   EXT   MORNING

The pickup is a tiny dot on the horizon.

ORTEGA and RICHARDSON give up and turn around.

PICKUP   INT   MORNING

JACK burns up another dirt road, surrounded by stands of tall Saguaros.

MOUNTAINS UP AHEAD.

RAVINE   INT   DAY

The pickup is parked in a wash.

JACK is on foot, headed up into the MOUNTAIN RANGE.

DESERT   EXT   DAY

JACK crosses a vast plateau, following two ruts of an ancient wagon trail.

He has no water.

Seated in the shade of a giant cactus, he cuts and peels a couple of prickly pears.

He eats the sweet fruit.

SAGUARO FOREST   EXT   DAY

JACK climbs uphill. His clothes are in tatters. He is unshaven, totally determined.

Military jets leave vapor trails overhead.

INDIAN RANCH   EXT   DAY

Bleating of goats.

JACK trudges past an old APACHE's trailer, with its pen of goats and cactus patch.

The APACHE is picking mice out of a little wire cage, holding them by their tails.

JACK points to a BRIGHT REFLECTION, glinting on the mountain.

                    JACK
          That Colonel Ames' place?

The APACHE nods, eyes invisible behind his shades.

                    JACK
               Thanks.

JACK heads on, up the hill.

Behind him, the APACHE drops the mice into a cage holding three rattlesnakes.

He sings an ancient song.

ELECTRIC FENCE   EXT   DAY

JACK follows an animal trail to the fence.

On the far side is the AMES HOUSE – its windows glowing like a wall of mirrors in the sun.

JACK's trail leads to a hole where the COYOTES have dug under the fence.

The carcass of a COYOTE lies nearby.

JACK crawls under the electric fence.

OUTSIDE THE MANSION WALL   EXT DAY

JACK threads his way through a cholla cactus patch.

He can hear SPLASHING in a pool.

He climbs the wall –

POOL   EXT   DAY

From the wall, JACK has a fantastic view of the desert he's just hiked through.

He drops down next to a glass table. A Premier smokeless cigarette burns in the ashtray. A half-empty whisky glass sits next to it.

The bottle and a black robe on the ground.

Suddenly, RUBY emerges from the pool. Beads of water glisten on her richly textured skin.

She is naked.

JACK watches as she flips over, her body and feet disappearing beneath the surface of the pool.

Silence, only water lapping.

VIDEO POV:

Of JACK, standing beside the pool.

SURVEILLANCE CENTER   INT   DAY

RANDY and TWO MEN with earphones watch JACK on the monitor.

POOL   EXT   DAY

JACK's eyes search the pool. RUBY surfaces again at the opposite end.
She paddles lazily on her back to the middle of the pool.

JACK sits down in a wrought-iron chair.

Flipping onto her belly, kicking smoothly, RUBY glides slowly towards JACK.

                    RUBY
          Why don't you just jump in?

In one fluid motion her hands push down on the pool rim and RUBY stands
beside the pool.

She wrings the water from her hair, staring at him with no expression.

VIDEO POV:

ZOOM IN ON JACK. He looks away, embarrassed.

POOL   EXT   DAY

RUBY walks to the ashtray, picks up the Premier, takes a drag –

                    RUBY
          You shouldn't be here.

                    JACK
          Who says so?

RUBY sits down opposite him in a lounge chair.

                    RUBY
          The Colonel. He's diagnosed you as
          a paranoid schizophrenic.

                    JACK
          Just because you're paranoid doesn't
          mean someone isn't out to get you.

                    RUBY
          That's very perceptive. But it won't play
          in the Colonel's world. The philosophy here
          is: 'Think positively, or not at all.'

She reaches for her drink.

                    JACK
          You didn't happen to know a policeman
          by the name of Bob Baxter, did you?

                    RUBY
                 (in a monotone)
          White male. Forty-six. Alcoholic.
          Advanced kidney deterioration.
          Failing eyesight. Family man.

JACK stares at her.

DR. NED MOUNT appears from within the house.

OPERATING ROOM   INT   DAY

The COLONEL is scrubbed and gowned and wearing a surgical mask.

He supervises a TEAM OF SURGEONS operating on a small body.

ANGLE ON RANDY

Tapping on the glass partition. An AIDE whispers to the COLONEL.

OUTER ROOM   INT   DAY

COLONEL AMES enters, pulling off his mask.

The big room is full of leather bound books, animal trophies, medical systems, computer gear.

RANDY points to the television set.

ON SCREEN:

JACK, RUBY and DR. NED MOUNT beside the pool.

                    DR. NED (on TV)
          Excuse me, Mr. Ditko, but may I ask
          what you're doing here?

                    JACK (on TV)
          I came to talk to Colonel Ames about
          that job he offered me.

                    DR. NED (on TV)
          I'm not aware of any job.

                    JACK (on TV)
          Head of Security.

The COLONEL frowns.

                    AMES
          Randy –

<u>POOL</u> EXT DAY

DR. NED throws the black kimono at RUBY.

                    DR. NED
               (to JACK)
          Wait here.
               (to RUBY)
          Put this on and come inside.

                    RUBY
          Fuck you, Dr. Ned.

                    DR. NED
          Ruby, this is for your own good! Your blood
          sugar is way up. You've been smoking again.
          If the Colonel ever –

                    RUBY
          You're the one who's going to have a massive
          coronary, Dr. Ned. I've seen your chart.
          You should be extremely quiet. No stress.
          Absolutely no sex. Eat a brown rice diet.

DR. NED is speechless.

                    RUBY
          Now run along.

DR. NED turns on his heels and exits.

                    RUBY
          Can you believe Dr. Ned? Woodrow has him
          squire me about so people won't think I'm
          with Woodrow.

                    JACK
          Are you?

                    RUBY
          Ruby Diamante is all things to all men.
          For you I'm going to be a source of good
          advice. Get out right now.

                    JACK
          I'm doing nothing wrong.

                    RUBY
          That's why you should get out.

                    JACK
          You ever see any Spanish kids up at the
          Center?

                    RUBY
          What Spanish kids? From Spain?

                    JACK
          What is the Colonel doing with all those
          kids up there?

                    RUBY
          What kids?

                    JACK
          The Spanish kids.

                    RUBY
          You mean the HISPANIC kids. The ones
          Chalo Quintana brought from Mexico.

                    JACK
          YES!

                    RUBY
          Using them as neomorts.

A long silence.

                    JACK
          What?

                    RUBY
          Neomorts. Harvestable organ banks
          or repositories. It's like a farm.

                    JACK
          A farm.

                    RUBY
          Yes. You know. A ranch. You have twelve
          cows. You get hungry. You eat one.
          You have twenty children from El Salvador.
          A rich kid in San Diego suffers third degree
          burns over most of her body. You take
          some Salvadoran skin and graft it on.
          Same with the organs. Hearts. Kidneys.
          Lungs. Liver. Neomorts.

RUBY dives in the pool.

A bird of prey calls.

A MAN in Acme Pool Services overalls walks up, dragging a heavy hosepipe.

                    POOL MAN
          Can you move, please? I have to put the
          CHLORINE in --

JACK shifts his chair –

The POOL MAN aims the hose, knocks off the valve.

A high-pressure jet of CHLORINATED WATER blasts JACK backwards into the pool.

UNDER WATER   EXT   DAY

JACK turns over and over in the water.

POOL   EXT   DAY

JACK surfaces, coughing. The HOSE hits him again.

RUBY swims to the other end of the pool.

UNDER WATER   EXT   DAY

JACK dives, trying to avoid the HOSE.

He surfaces again.

The HOSE turns him upside down.

He starts to drown.

POOL   EXT   DAY

RANDY and the MEN with earphones drag JACK out of the pool.

RUBY, wrapped in a towel, heads for the house.

OPERATING ROOM   INT   DAY

 JACK is strapped to a gurney and hooked up to various machines.
He sweats and shakes.

ANGLE ON DR. NED MOUNT

Shooting JACK up with sodium pentathol.

JACK'S POV: RANDY, DR. NED, and COLONEL AMES.

His vision is blurred – the others constantly appear at different distances,
in different costumes.

                    DR. NED
          Will you count to ten for me, please?

                    JACK
          One ... two ... three ...

RANDY punches JACK in the face.

                    RANDY
          Where's Angela Quintana?

                    JACK
          I ... she ...
               (fighting the truth serum)
          She ... doesn't love me ...

The COLONEL studies JACK's statistics on the computer monitor.

                         AMES
What an appalling life style these cops
have. Liver porous. Heart that of a 90-year
old. Kidneys shot with booze. Lungs black
with tar. It could cost over two million
dollars to get him fixed up.

                         RANDY
                  (yelling at JACK)
Tell us where the woman is!

                         JACK
Fuck you...

                         DR. NED
Jack ... you're not well. We're doctors.
You must be truthful with us or we won't
be able to help you.

                         AMES
His face is asymetrical. I'll bet he had a
small stroke, when he was a baby.

                         JACK
                  (shouting through the drugs)
MURDERERS!!!

JACK passes out.

                         DR. NED
Let's give him another fifteen mils.

COLONEL AMES shakes his head. He nods to RANDY.

                         AMES
Get rid of him.

DESERT   EXT   NIGHT

A BONFIRE is tended by the COLONEL'S MEN.

RANDY and the POOL MAN drag JACK about among the CACTUS.

They are illuminated by the headlights of a pickup truck.

All hold tall boys of beer.

RANDY throws JACK down beside the BONFIRE.

JACK is still drugged and badly bruised. He has a spiked finger of CHOLLA
stuck to his face.

                         RANDY
               Whooeee! Bing, toss me a beer!

JACK's hand falls in the fire.

                         POOL MAN
               Get his hand out of the fire.

                         RANDY
               What for? We're here to party.
                         (sings)
               Here's to good friends;
               Tonight is something special –

He pulls back the hammer of his pistol, aims it at JACK's head.

The POOL MAN kicks JACK's hand out of the fire.

                         POOL MAN
               Smells like barbecue.

A red laser light dot appears on the forehead of the third man, BING.

PTHWUT!

A HOLE appears in BING's head. He falls into the fire.

RANDY and the POOL MAN freeze.

The red dot centers on the POOL MAN's chest.

PTHWUT!

The POOL MAN falls; RANDY dives for the door of the truck.

PTHWUT! PTHWUT! Two more bullets take out the pickup's headlights.

RANDY is in the cab, gunning the motor.

The pickup truck reverses, engine screaming, into the night.

                         POOL MAN
               Randy, don't leave me! RA –

PTHWUT!

The POOL MAN falls silent.

The sound of the pickup dies away.

JACK lies on his back. He reaches into the burning man's pocket and finds
a PACKET OF CIGARETTES.

Footsteps approach.

O'BRIEN arrives. He carries the AR-15 sniper's rifle and wears night vision goggles.

> O'BRIEN
>> Hi.

> JACK
>> Hi.

JACK tries to light up. His hands are shaking. His right hand is badly burned.

O'BRIEN takes the cigarette from JACK and lights it in the fire.

He takes out his comb and deftly extracts the CHOLLA from JACK's face.

> O'BRIEN
> It's lucky for you you're on drugs...

O'BRIEN relieves the corpses of their guns – a .38 automatic, a "street sweeper"
scatter gun.

> O'BRIEN
>> Want one?

> JACK
>> The .38.

JACK sticks the gun in his belt.

> O'BRIEN
> Can you walk?

O'BRIEN offers him an arm. JACK gets up on his own.

DESERT GRAVE SITE   EXT   NIGHT

COYOTES have dug up the recently-leveled ground.

O'BRIEN shines a flashlight into the shallow grave, illuminating little bones.

JACK takes a slug from a bottle of mescal. A coyote howls.

> O'BRIEN
> It's been going on for about ten years.
> Quintana drove 'em up at first. Now they
> fly 'em into military bases. The Colonel's
> well-connected – used to be an Army
> surgeon – so ...

JACK examines one of the SMALL SKELETONS in the grave.

> JACK
> What about their parents ... ?

> O'BRIEN
> Most of 'em are street kids. Niños de la
> Calle. They promise 'em five hundred
> dollars and a ticket to the US. Know
> what that means to somebody in
> Honduras, Guatemala?

JACK straightens, staring at the grave.

> O'BRIEN
> And so they get here, and the Colonel
> takes a kidney. He keeps 'em at his
> Health Center, stoned on drugs. Till he
> needs a liver donor ... You only got one
> liver, right?
> (points to the grave)
> Then it's here.

O'BRIEN looks at JACK. JACK is shaking as he comes off the drugs.

> O'BRIEN
> You want something for that?

O'BRIEN pulls a handful of pills from his pocket.

JACK draws the .38, left-handed. He points it at O'BRIEN's head.

> JACK
> Who the fuck ARE you, mister?
> I don't recall hearing your NAME.

> O'BRIEN
> My name is Alejandro O'Brien. I am a private
> investigator from Guadalajara, Mexico.
> Angela Quintana hired me to investigate   [CONT.]

                    O'BRIEN   [CONT.]
          her husband's death. She know what I
          would find out, of course. And that I would
          have no choice ...

JACK is taken aback.

                    JACK
          You were on the golf course. You killed
          Ames' business associate.

                    O'BRIEN
          I did. And next time I'll kill Ames.

                    JACK
          What's in it for you?

                    O'BRIEN
          What do you mean? This man is worse
          than a monster. These are my people's
          children. I have no choice.
               (eyes on the grave)
          They must all be buried now.

O'BRIEN disappears into the darkness.

He returns with a shovel. Starts to dig.

<u>SILVERBELL ROAD</u>   EXT   MORNING

O'BRIEN's LTD pulls up outside a Cafe-Bar on the outskirts of town.

<u>BAR</u>   INT   MORNING

JACK and O'BRIEN enter the bar.

Light pours through the ceiling. MEN on ladders are knocking a big hole in
the roof, kicking up dust and letting DAYLIGHT in –

ANGELA steps into the light.

                    BARMAN
          Dos cervezas, Jack?

                    JACK
          Tres.

ANGELA embraces O'BRIEN, staring over his shoulder at JACK.

                         O'BRIEN
               We're going after the kids.

                         ANGELA
               Not without the Colonel.

                         O'BRIEN
               Second on the list.

Impassive, JACK picks up his beer and drinks.

He takes a set of car keys from a hook behind the bar.

                         JACK
                    (to the BARMAN)
               I'm borrowing your station wagon, Mike.

                         BARMAN
               Great.

                         JACK
                    (to ANGELA and O'BRIEN)
               Don't get too comfortable. I'll be back
               in an hour.

We follow JACK out of the bar into the –

CAFE   INT   MORNING

– in front. People eating breakfast stare at JACK's ripped clothes, bruised face,
and charred and blistered hand.

JACK steps into the pay phone booth.

He dials a number, drops in two dimes.

                         JACK
               Jack Ditko for Detective Ortega.

                         ORTEGA'S VOICE
               Jack, where the hell are you?
               You're in big trouble!

                         JACK
               You've got to help me. You and
               Richardson.

<u>TPD</u>   INT   MORNING

DETECTIVE ORTEGA sits at his desk.

At the next desk, the COMMISSIONER and DETECTIVE RICHARDSON
listen on extension phones.

>   ORTEGA
>   (into phone)
> Charley isn't going to help you, Jack.
> You're wanted for bumping off a transient
> at the Renaissance Inn.

>   JACK'S VOICE
> What? Who??

>   ORTEGA
> Bodybuilder by the name of Floyd
> Hargreaves. Somebody shot him with
> your gun.

<u>PHONE BOOTH</u>   INT   MORNING

JACK is incensed.

>   JACK
> Listen, Hargreaves was killed two days
> ago on Colonel Ames' Golf Course, along
> with the Turkish dude –

>   ORTEGA'S VOICE
> What Turkish dude? What the hell are
> you talking about?

>   JACK
> Someone is trying to set me up because
> I'm onto something REAL BIG, Jaime.
> And you and Charley are the only guys
> I trust.

<u>TPD</u>   INT   MORNING

DETECTIVE ORTEGA rolls his eyes.

>   ORTEGA
> Where are you, Jack?

                    JACK'S VOICE
          I want you both to meet me at the airplane
          graveyard in two hours. I'll be waiting between
          the DC-7s and the DC-8's. Just you two guys.
          Alone. No surprises.

The COMMISSIONER nods to ORTEGA to agree.

                    ORTEGA
          You got it, buddy.

JACK hangs up the phone.

<u>JACK'S PLACE</u>   EXT   MORNING

JACK drives up in the BARMAN's old station wagon.

<u>JACK'S PLACE</u>   INT   MORNING

He puts on a clean white shirt.

He takes the Chinese hand grenade from the shelf and hooks it on his belt.

Retrieves his 30.30 from beneath the bed.

Takes a slug from the bottle of mescal.

Groans and sits down.

JACK sits very still, centering his energy.

<u>JACK'S PLACE</u>   EXT   MORNING

Burned, and unshaven, carrying the bottle and his rifle, JACK emerges from the
house.

His wife – JO ANN – sits at the wheel of a brand new Suburban. Their sixteen year
old daughter – STACEY – sits beside her. A horse trailer is rigged up behind.

JO ANN stares at JACK and shakes her head.

                    JO ANN
          What party have you been to?

JACK goes to the station wagon, throws the rifle in the back.

JO ANN gets out of the truck. STACEY stays inside, turning up the radio.

> JO ANN
> Someone called the house looking for you.
> Said you better leave town right away.

> JACK
> Who was it?

> JO ANN
> I don't know. Stacey talked to him.

JACK knocks on the window of the Suburban.

STACEY lower the window.

> JACK
> Turn it down.

Reluctantly, she turns it down.

> JACK
> Who was it that called?

> STACEY
> A man.

> JACK
> What'd he say?

> STACEY
> He said you were going to be accused of
> murdering someone and that it had to do
> with drugs. He said you should get out of
> town. Right away.

> JACK
> Did the man have an accent?
> Did he talk like a Mexican?

> STACEY
> He talked like a cop. You all talk the same.
> Stupid. I was really scared, Dad.

> JACK
> I know you were, baby. Don't you worry
> about me.

                    STACEY
          I'm not, Dad. I'm worried about me and Mom.
          You don't even have a job and now you're
          involved in drug dealing.

                    JACK
          You believe that?

                    STACEY
          No, not really. But I know that you're
          fucked up. And if you get killed it'll be
          really fucked.

                    JACK
          Don't talk that way around your mother.

STACEY groans.

                    JO ANN
          Look, Jack, if you're thinking of skipping town
          you need to settle up with me.

                    JACK
          I'm not thinking of skipping town.

                    JO ANN
          You're five months behind. I've been good
          about it but I can't carry you forever.

                    JACK
          You're not CARRYING me. What about that
          jewelry designer you live with? Why doesn't
          he pay something?

                    JO ANN
          You're my husband. Dennis isn't. You're her
          father. Dennis isn't. You get the difference?

STACEY groans again.

                    STACEY
          Oh, pul...eeze!

She winds up the window. Turns on the music. Loud.

WIDE ANGLE

JACK, JO ANN and STACEY and the big Suburban are all very small against
the morning sky.

JACK and JO ANN shout curses at each other.

HIGHWAY   EXT   DAY

ANGELA drives the station wagon into the desert. JACK beside her.

O'BRIEN in the back, checking his guns.

                    ANGELA
          We'll need another vehicle. We'll be
          followed. We'll lay low this side of the
          border, cross over in a couple of days...

SWAP MEET   EXT   DAY

O'BRIEN buys an airbrushed CHOLO VAN. It sports a mural of the Flag, the Snake,
JUAREZ, and the VIRGIN MARY.

ANGELA and JACK drive off in the station wagon.

SPORTING GOODS STORE   EXT   DAY

JACK and ANGELA load tents, sleeping bags, fishing rods and a cooler into
the back of the station wagon.

AIRPLANE GRAVEYARD   EXT   DAY

RICHARDSON and ORTEGA wait between the DC-7's and the DC-8's.

DC-8   INT   DAY

POLICE COMMISSIONER GARRETT sits in the burned-out airplane hull,
listening to the DETECTIVES' wire taps.

PULL BACK to reveal a black-clad S.W.A.T. TEAM, armed with M-16s, ready
to burst out of the cargo doors.

AIRPLANE GRAVEYARD   EXT   DAY

RICHARDSON and ORTEGA continue to wait.

ORTEGA looks at his watch.

                    ORTEGA
          Jack's never late. Something's off.

                  RICHARDSON
          Know what I think?

                    ORTEGA
          Maybe my watch is off.
          That might be his car, over there!

                  RICHARDSON
          We're fucked. We're really fucked.

REGENCY CENTER   EXT   DAY

Tranquility reigns. Golf karts roll to and fro.

RANDY strolls the grounds with an earphone.

On the hill behind him, TWO FIGURES wearing white coats head for
the windowless adobe...

WINDOWLESS ADOBE   INT   DAY

JACK and O'BRIEN walk down a long corridor. They wear white doctors'
coats. JACK wears a false mustache. O'BRIEN wears thick horn rim glasses.

O'BRIEN tries a door. It's locked. He picks the lock.

ROOM   INT   DAY

An ancient WOMAN sits upright in a bed. She's attached to various life
support systems. On a tray are several birthday cards.

                  OLD WOMAN
          It's my birthday!

                JACK AND O'BRIEN
          Happy birthday!

They leave the room.

CORRIDOR   INT   DAY

JACK backs away. Follows O'BRIEN into –

<u>DORMITORY</u>   INT   DAY

- where TEN LATINO KIDS play on the floor.

Around them is an expensive array of toys, including superhero capes and a huge Mexican sombrero.

The KIDS are obviously sedated. They wear green smocks.

Among them are LUIS, ERIBERTO, and CARMEN.

ERIBERTO wears an eye patch.

                    O'BRIEN
              (to the KIDS, in Spanish)
          Where are the others?

                    ERIBERTO
              (in Spanish)
          There are no others. We're all that's left.

The KIDS start screaming. JACK is paralyzed.

                    JACK
          Make 'em stop screaming!

                    O'BRIEN
          How the hell do I do that?

                    JACK
              Just do it!

                    O'BRIEN
              (to the KIDS, in Spanish)
          Don't worry, children. We're only playing.
          You know Superman, don't you? This
          Americano is Superman and he's come to
          save you!

The KIDS look wide eyed from JACK to the large poster of SUPERMAN and BATMAN on the wall, between COOL MOE E and a sketch of PANCHO VILLA.

                    ERIBERTO
          El no es Superman. No tiene musculos.

                    LUIS
          El es mas como Pancho Villa.

                    OTHER KIDS
          Es mas como JOHN-BOY WALTON -
          - o Don Johnson - CORRUPCION EN
          MIAMI!

O'BRIEN takes the sombrero from the wall and puts it on JACK's head.

                    O'BRIEN
               (in Spanish)
          You see? He IS Pancho Villa AND
          Superman AND John-Boy at the same
          time! Like in the Bible!

The KIDS laugh.

                    KIDS
          Pancho! Pancho!

                    JACK
          What are you saying?

                    O'BRIEN
          I'n telling them you're Pancho Villa.
               (to ERIBERTO)
          De donde eres?

                    ERIBERTO
          Zacatecas.

                    O'BRIEN
               (in Spanish)
          Do you want Pancho Villa to take you
          back to Zacatecas?

                    ERIBERTO
          SI!

                    O'BRIEN
          Vamos, pues! Let's go!

CORRIDOR   INT   DAY

JACK and O'BRIEN lead the TEN KIDS down the hall.

The ELEVATOR DOORS open - RUBY is within -

She stares wide-eyed as JACK and O'BRIEN herd the yelling KIDS into the
elevator. The doors close.

<u>ELEVATOR</u> INT DAYLIGHT

There are only TWO BUTTONS on the panel.

JACK presses the lower one.

> RUBY
> (to ERIBERTO, in Spanish)
> Where are you going with these crazies?

> ERIBERTO
> (in Spanish)
> They say they're taking us back to Mexico.
> That one thinks he's Pancho Villa.

> RUBY
> I guess that explains the hand grenade.

JACK pulls his doctor's coat over the hand grenade hooked to his belt.

The elevator stops and the door opens to an –

<u>UNDERGROUND GARAGE</u> INT DAYLIGHT

DR. RUTH BENWAY and an AIDE are waiting for the elevator.

> DR. BENWAY
> Ruby, what are you doing with these
> children? They don't go out. You should
> know better.

> JACK
> We're taking them to play some ball.

> DR. BENWAY
> That's absurd.
> (to AIDE)
> Call Security!

> RUBY
> Don't do it! They've got a bomb! They're
> threatening to blow up the Center!

O'BRIEN pulls his gun.

JACK, one step behind, reveals the grenade.

DR. BENWAY and the AIDE back away.

                    RUBY
         Don't use your radio! You'll set the bomb off!

JACK marches RUBY towards the parked ambulances.

O'BRIEN herds the KIDS behind them.

ANGELA is waiting in an ambulance.

                    RUBY
         Angela? Oh shit!

DR. BENWAY and the AIDE pile into the elevator. The door closes.

                    ANGELA
         Jack! What are you doing with THIS?

                    JACK
         She's with us.

                    ANGELA
         No she's not. She belongs to the Colonel.

                    RUBY
         Fuck you, Angela! I don't belong to anyone!

JACK pushes RUBY into the ambulance.

O'BRIEN directs the last of the KIDS into the back.

The KIDS are having a great time.

REGENCY CLINIC   EXT   DAY

The ambulance bursts out of the underground garage and hurtles down
the driveway.

RANDY runs out of the Clinic.

DR. NED MOUNT, driving into work, wheels his car around –

AMBULANCE   INT   DAY

ANGELA pilots the ambulance through the gate.

TEN KIDS are shouting in back.

                    ANGELA
                 Is the Colonel dead?

                    O'BRIEN
                 He wasn't there!

                     KIDS
              Andale, Don Johnson! MAS RAPIDO!

JACK lets go of RUBY's arm –

RUBY dives for the door handle, opening the door –

ANGELA accelerates and swings the wheel –

DITCH   EXT   DAY

– sending the ambulance off the road and down a steep grade.

RUBY is almost thrown out. JACK pulls her in again.

They pull up next to MIKE the BARMAN's station wagon.

CLINIC ROAD   EXT   DAY

DR. NED's convertible, with RANDY at the wheel, tears past.

In the distance – approaching police car bubbles.

The old station wagon, its windows obscured by reflective pictures of an
Arizona sunset, pulls onto the road –

– ignored by everyone.

STATION WAGON   INT   DAYLIGHT

Fourteen people on board. RUBY squeezed in among the KIDS.

JACK finds a Norteño station.

ARROYO   EXT   DAYLIGHT

On the edge of the city, all fourteen climb stiffly out of the station wagon,
beneath a bridge where O'BRIEN's LTD is parked..

O'BRIEN unlocks the CHOLO VAN –

– the KIDS pile in, start checking out the camping gear and cooler.

RUBY runs away.

JACK grabs her. They both fall down, JACK screaming as he lands on his bad hand.

ANGELA aims her gun at RUBY.

                         ANGELA
          I'll just shoot her in the foot, so she can't
          follow us.

BANG!

A bullet ricochets off concrete, near RUBY's head.

                         RUBY
          Don't let her kill me, you idiots!

O'BRIEN dives for ANGELA, tackling her.

The wrestle in the dust.

He wrenches the gun away from her.

The CHILDREN climb out of the van.

Some whimper, others run around shouting.

                         JACK
                (yelling at the children)
          Get the fuck back in the van!

TWO KIDS being to cry.

ANGELA crawls over to RUBY and slugs her on the jaw.

JACK fires his pistol in the air.   Everyone freezes.

ANGLE ON ERIBERTO AND LUIS

                         ERIBERTO
                (in Spanish)
          If this get's any crazier, let's run for it.

                         LUIS
          I'll drive the van.

ANGLE ON JACK

Lowering the gun.

                    JACK
          No one is to touch this girl.
          She's under my protection.

                    ANGELA
          Kill the little slut, O'Brien.
          Then we'll get the Colonel.

ANGLE ON O'BRIEN

Thinking it over.

                    RUBY
          You don't want to murder me. Here's why:
          I have the entire operation in my head.
          Budget. Marketing. Account numbers.
          International contact sheet. Alive, I can
          be a lot of help to you.

ANGELA stares at RUBY, computing.

                    O'BRIEN
          It's not important. Cut off the head,
          the body dies.

                    RUBY
          But that's not what Angela wants. She
          wants to take over, right, Angela?

                    ANGELA
          You little whore. If either of you had any
          balls you'd blow her lying head off.
          Right now.

O'BRIEN rises. He walks to the station wagon and extracts his golf bag.
Heads for the LTD.

                    ANGELA
          Where do you think you're going?

                    O'BRIEN
          Back to the Clinic.

                    JACK
          O'Brien, don't do it.

                    RUBY
You're wasting your time. Woodrow's not there.
          (they all turn to stare at her)
At times like this, he holes up at the big house.
Takes the carrier bag full of money out of the big
safe. And makes impromptu travel plans.

                    JACK
How much money is in that carrier bag?

                    RUBY
About five million dollars.

                    ANGELA
Cash?

                    RUBY
Four million in cash. The rest in bonds.
A little gold.

                    O'BRIEN
Let's kill him at his house.

ANGELA nods.

                    ANGELA
Five million dollars, split three ways.

JACK takes RUBY by the arm and, whistling, heads for the CHOLO VAN,
never entirely turning his back on ANGELA and O'BRIEN.

                    JACK
              (to the CHILDREN)
Vamos muchachos! Vamos a Mexico!

He herds the KIDS inside. O'BRIEN follows him.

                    O'BRIEN
One third of that money, Jack, would feed
a lot of kids. Two thirds would feed twice
as many.

                    JACK
You take care of that, pal.
I'm goin' to Mexico.

He helps RUBY into the front seat.

O'BRIEN extends his left hand.

O'BRIEN

In all my life I have only met three men
I admire more.

JACK and O'BRIEN shake hands firmly.

ANGELA takes off in the station wagon. O'BRIEN follows in the LTD.

JACK slides in behind the wheel of the van. RUBY is totally confused.

<u>VAN</u>   INT   DAY

JACK drives. RUBY sits next to him, staring straight ahead.

RUBY

I don't get it. Where are we going?

JACK

I told you. Mexico.

RUBY

You mean you weren't kidding? I thought
you were going to circle back around, and
ambush the pair of them. Then ransom
me back to Woodrow. You mean I had it
all wrong?

JACK

Yeah. You did.

RUBY

Aren't you interested in money?

JACK

Not that much.

RUBY

(stunned)
Very interesting.

CARMEN starts to cry again.

JACK

What's the matter with her?

RUBY

You lost your mustache.

<u>CANYON</u>   EXT AFTERNOON

The VAN is parked by a stream.

JACK shows the CHILDREN how to set up tents beneath the shade trees.

RUBY leans against a tree, rubbing her jaw.

> RUBY
> A specialist should take a look at my
> metatarsal.

> JACK
> You bet. Tomorrow morning, after we're
> across the border.

> RUBY
> Right. I'll bet you're thinking about driving
> to some big Mexican town and turning
> these kids over to the authorities.

> JACK
> Could be.

> RUBY
> At some point soon after you do that,
> you and these children will be killed.
> The Colonel is more powerful than you
> can imagine.

> JACK
> And you're a sicko. How can you live with
> somebody who murders children?

> RUBY
> Woodrow is my husband. We were married
> when I was fifteen. A Hopi ceremony.
> He's done good as well as evil. He's saved
> a lot of lives. He saved Elvis Presley
> more than once!

> JACK
> That doesn't mean anything.

> RUBY
> I know.

They stare at the CHILDREN.

                         RUBY
          I was one of these kids. You should meet
          the parents of the children that get the
          livers and the eyes. They're nice people.
          They never ask where the donations
          come from. It's complex...

LUIS comes up.

                         LUIS
                    (in Spanish)
          Hey, Ruby. Is it true this dude is Pancho Villa?

                         ERIBERTO
                    (in Spanish)
          And is he really going to take us all back to
          the cities we came from?

                         JACK
          What do they want?

                         RUBY
          They want to know if you are really going to
          take them back to Mexico.

                         JACK
          Tell 'em yes.

The CHILDREN understand, and cheer. CARMEN whispers to RUBY.

                         RUBY
          Well, several of them would prefer to live
          together with you, on your RANCH.

                         JACK
          Tell 'em as long as they're with Pancho,
          they're welcome anytime.

RUBY looks away, suddenly depressed.

RAILROAD CROSSING   EXT   NIGHT

A PATROL CAR has pulled over the station wagon.

A COP gives ANGELA the drunk test.

                    COP
              (into radio)
     Clocked her doing a hundred and ten on the
     off-ramp. It's the Quintana woman, yeah.
     Want us to bring her to the Federal Building
     or book her?

               GARRETT'S VOICE
              (via radio)
     This is Police Commissioner Garrett.
     Bring her to my office right away –

The COPS exchange a glance.

LTD   INT   NIGHT

O'BRIEN is parked a hundred yards behind the cop car.

The COPS put ANGELA in the back of their patrol car and drive off.

O'BRIEN follows.

CANYON   EXT   NIGHT

JACK sits by the stream. A campfire next to him.

The CHILDREN are asleep. RUBY stares at the sky.

JACK starts to load his rifle.

                    RUBY
     Going back to see the Colonel?

                    JACK
     I'm going to offer him a deal. Your life
     for the kids'.

                    RUBY
     What do you propose to do about the
     children while you're gone?

                    JACK
     Well, I propose that you look after 'em.
     If I'm not back by nightfall tomorrow,
     take 'em to the Sheriff in Bisbee.
     He's a friend of mine.

                    RUBY
          This plan is worse than your last one.
          Woodrow will kill you. The Sheriff will
          turn the kids over to the Border Patrol.

                    JACK
          At least they'll get home.

                    RUBY
          Goodbye.

JACK nods. He heads for the VAN.

CARMEN runs after JACK, holding his Pancho Villa hat.

                    CARMEN
          Su sombrero, Pancho.

JACK solemnly takes the sombrero. Formally, he salutes CARMEN and puts it on.
He gest into the van.

Trying not to wake the CHILDREN, he takes off the handbrake. Lets the van roll
quietly downhill.

ANGLE ON ERIBERTO AND LUIS

Running after the van and climbing on the chrome-plated ladder that leads
to the roof rack.

<u>SAGUARO ROAD</u>   EXT   NIGHT

COMISSIONER GARRETT's sedan heads down the saguaro road to COLONEL AMES'
MANSION.

GARRETT drives. In the back, ANGELA sits with RANDY.

<u>COLONEL'S COURTYARD</u>   EXT   NIGHT

Totem poles, Chac Mools and Incan idols are on display.

RANDY and GARRETT march ANGELA towards the house.

TWO AUTOMATIC GATES swing shut in the electric fence.

PROFUSION of ARMED GUARDS beside the COLONEL's stretch limo.

<u>GREAT ROOM, COLONEL'S MANSION</u>   INT   NIGHT

RANDY and GARRETT present ANGELA to COLONEL AMES.

DR. NED mixes martinis. DR. BENWAY sits reading an anatomy book.

                    AMES
          Damn you, Angela. Where's my Ruby?

                    ANGELA
          I don't know, Woodrow. I think that cop
          took her to Mexico.

                    AMES
          You never should have come back.
          I warned you. That was a stupid move,
          killing Mustafa.

                    ANGELA
          I was just evening up the score. You're the
          stupid one, thinking you could cut me out
          by killing Chalo and hiring that fucking
          Turkish quack to replace us –

                    AMES
          It was business, Angela. Mustafa cut me
          a better deal. He would have opened up the
          Middle East, India...

DR. NED approaches with the cocktail shaker.

                    DR. NED
          Anyone for a martini?

                    DR. BENWAY
          Mrs. Quintana, when did you last see this
          cop who has the children?

                    ANGELA
          A couple hours ago. Heading south on 19.

                    AMES
          Seal the border.

                    GARRETT
          I'll do my best –

                    AMES
          Do better.

GARRETT picks up the phone, dials.

AMES reaches out a bony arm, strokes ANGELA's cheek.

ANGELA turns her head away.

>   AMES
>   Two hours ago. Hmm. What exactly have
>   you been doing for the last two hours?

>   ANGELA
>   Driving around. Thinking about how much
>   I hate you.

>   AMES
>   Dear Angela. One thing I can always count
>   on is that you always lie. And that you're
>   always up to something. You let yourself
>   get arrested, but no one knows where your
>   two partners are. I don't believe Ditko's
>   left town at all. I think he's RIGHT HERE.
>   (snaps his fingers)
>   Sodium Pentathol.

DR. NED produces a syringe.

>   GARRETT
>   The phone's dead –

COLONEL'S COURTYARD   EXT NIGHT

The COMMISSIONER'S CAR explodes.

Burning wreckage flies in all directions.

The mansion lights go out.

GREAT ROOM, COLONEL'S MANSION   INT NIGHT

In darkness, ANGELA kicks DR. NED on his shins.

DR. NED drops his syringe.

COLONEL'S COURTYARD   EXT NIGHT

GUARDS run everywhere, waving flashlights –

VOICES
Get the generator going!
Let's have some light out here!

The generator starts up. Lights come back on.

The fence gates open automatically --

GUARD
Not the gate! Close it!

- revealing TWO DEAD GUARDS lying outside. Bullet holes in their foreheads.

A red laser light flickers across the mansion wall.

ANGLE ON THE SHOCKED FACES

of the SURVIVING GUARDS.

COLONEL'S MANSION   EXT   MORNING

The MANSION glitters in the first light of day.

JACK waits behind the wheel of the van, smoking his last cigarette.

CRANE UP TO REVEAL

ERIBERTO and LUIS

Sitting on the roof rack, smoking cigarettes.

JACK finishes his smoke, drives up the Saguaro Road.

SHOWDOWN MUSIC.

COLONEL'S COURTYARD   EXT   MORNING

VULTURES take off as the van enters through the open gates.

Dead GUARDS lie all around.

The COLONEL's limo is upside down, a bullet hole in the windshield.

COMMISSIONER GARRETT hangs in his seat belt, dead behind the wheel.

RANDY, gut shot, lying behind a Mayan trough, watches JACK approach
the mansion.

POOL   EXT   MORNING

JACK walks around the back of the house.

DR. BENWAY floats, face down, in the pool.

JACK cautiously approaches the windows of the –

GREAT ROOM   INT   MORNING

BULLET HOLES have been drilled through the big windows.

A glass bookcase lies shattered on the marble floor.
A piano slumps to one side, having lost a leg.

Kachina dolls and Kwakiutl death masks lie scattered next to Western art books
and a broken golf club.

DR. NED MOUNT lies on the couch, in shock, a pool of blood spreading over his linen
suit. A MACHINE PISTOL lies on the rug near his feet.

ANGLE ON JACK

Watching through the window as O'BRIEN presses a gun to COLONEL AMES' head.

                    AMES
              (in a monotone)
          4 left. 16 right. 7 left. 1 right.

ANGLE ON ANGELA

Shot in the leg, leaning against the wall, spinning the combination to the safe.

                    AMES
              That's it.

The safe opens. ANGELA takes out a case and opens it.

It is full of MONEY, GOLD, and TREASURY BILLS.

                    ANGELA
              Thank you, Woodrow.
                 (to O'BRIEN)
              Kill him.

JACK enters the room with his .38 drawn.

The COLONEL looks up, angrily.

                    AMES
          Where's my wife, Ditko?

                    JACK
          Everyone freeze.

O'BRIEN and ANGELA do so. DR. NED groans, weekly.

                    JACK
          Put the gun down, O'Brien. You too, Angela.
          Drop what's in your hands.

                    ANGELA
          Oh, Jack. Spare us the naive proposal that
          we turn Woodrow and his money in,
          march him up the steps of City Hall over
          the dead body of the Police Commissioner.
          That's not a happening option.

                    JACK
               (not wanting to think about it)
          Shut up.
               (to O'BRIEN)
          I told you to put that gun down.

O'BRIEN lowers his pistol but doesn't put it down.

                    O'BRIEN
          Sure, Jack. Let's all be real cool.

THE COLONEL stares fixedly at DR. NED.

DR. NED manages to return his gaze. COLONEL AMES directs DR. NED with his
eyes to the MACHINE PISTOL on the floor.

                    AMES
          Well, Ditko, I must hand it to you.
          You're a regular Lone Ranger.

JACK covers O'BRIEN, ANGELA and the COLONEL with his gun.

ANGELA sinks to the floor, her back to the wall.

                    AMES
          When you walked in, I thought you'd come
          to kill me, too –

He stares at DR. NED, reaching painfully for the MACHINE PISTOL.

                              JACK
                         I had it in mind –

                              AMES
                         Of course you did –

The COLONEL fixes JACK in the gleam of his ageless eyes.

                              ANGELA
                         Jack, he's got a gun!

ANGLE ON DR. NED

Falling on the MACHINE PISTOL.

ANGLE ON O'BRIEN

Shooting DR. NED.

ANGLE ON JACK

Firing at O'BRIEN.

ANGLE ON DR. NED

Convulsing as he lifts the gun, shooting ANGELA and O'BRIEN.

ANGLE ON COLONEL AMES

Diving through the melee –

ANGLE ON ANGELA

Dropping the bag, opening fire on JACK.

<u>OUTSIDE THE MANSION</u>   EXT   DAYLIGHT

ERIBERTO and LUIS watch through the big glass windows.

They see JACK and O'BRIEN take cover behind the piano.

They see the COLONEL come flying through the glass – his shirt pulled up,
revealing MANY OPERATION SCARS and FRESH STITCHES – running for
the COURTYARD.

<u>COURTYARD</u>   EXT   DAY

Dust blows. Death everywhere. Burned out cars.

COLONEL AMES walks forward, as if in a dream, looking for an AIDE, a GUARD, a vehicle...

                         RANDY
                Take the limo, Colonel...

RANDY, dying, sits on the wreckage of the limo. He aims his rifle –

<u>GREAT ROOM</u>   INT   DAY

Gunfire inside and outside.

JACK shelters behind the piano. O'BRIEN is hit.

                         O'BRIEN
                       (dying)
                Promise me one thing, Jack.

JACK looks down at him.

                         O'BRIEN
                Take the kids back. Every one. To his own home.

JACK winces.

                         JACK
                No problema.

                         O'BRIEN
                Also ... in Monterrey, there is a bartender ...
                I owe him ... fifty bucks ...

He dies. From across the room, ANGELA's voice is heard.

                         ANGELA
                Is he dead?
                       (JACK does not answer)
                Can you imagine: he wanted to give his share
                to the homeless. To charity. To all those kids.
                He must have had a guilty conscience.

ANGLE ON ANGELA

Wounded, painfully gathering up the money, stuffing it back into its bag.

                         ANGELA
                Are you dead, Jack?

                    JACK'S VOICE
                (from behind the piano)
            Not hardly...

ANGELA pumps the rest of the rest of the clip into the piano.

Strings pop. Ivory keys fly off.

JACK is showered with wood and metal.

ANGELA puts a fresh ammo clip into her pistol.

                    ANGELA
            Still alive?
                (no answer)
            I'll bet you are.

ANGLE ON JACK

Behind the piano. Wounded in the shoulder and his good arm, he tries to lift
the revolver. Neither hand can hold it.

                    ANGELA
            You know, Jack – it is JACK, isn't it? -
            of all the guys I've ever known, you're
            the first I ever thought I could – you know -
            run off to an ISLAND with. You don't want
            to do that, do you?
                (no answer)
            Oh, Jack. You're an all right guy, but you're
            not really a PLAYER.

BANG! Another bullet hole appears in the piano.

ANGLE ON ANGELA

Bleeding badly, crawling around the couch for an unobstructed view of JACK.

She holds her pistol with both hands.

ANGLE ON JACK

Pulling the Chinese hand grenade from his belt.

He tosses the grenade in ANGELA's direction.

She ducks, and JACK leaps out of the shattered window --

POOL SIDE   EXT   DAY

– and rolls away from the Great Room.

He hides behind a stone bench. There is no explosion.

                    ANGELA'S VOICE
          It was a DUD, Jack! Just like you...

GREAT ROOM   INT   DAY

ANGELA cradles the case of money, gold and bonds. She cannot rise.

                    ANGELA
          Jack, I can't see. You're not going to leave me,
          are you?

POOL SIDE   EXT   DAY

JACK gets painfully to his feet, and walks towards an arroyo –

                    ANGELA'S VOICE
          I've got the money! More than we expected.
          Much more. Jack..

ARROYO   EXT   DAY

The COLONEL lies in the arroyo. Around him, parts of an old rusted Chevy, a broken gurney and a busted box spring.

ERIBERTO and LUIS sit under a Saguaro, watching him.

                    AMES
          Remove the sacra ... improve on the natural
          world ... replace it entirely!
                    (yelling)
          Try to arrive at a solution to the problem you
          are IN! Not some preconceived idea ... that ...

He coughs, blood dribbling from his mouth.

                    AMES
          A future ... youth ... we're all ... cockroaches
          ... comrades in the war against death! And I'm --
          YES! ... the experiment is a complete success.

JACK arrives.

He stands beside the KIDS, watching the COLONEL die.

COLONEL'S COURTYARD   EXT   DAY

JACK speaks into the radio of COMMISSIONER GARRETT's upside-down sedan.

>   JACK
>   (into radio)
>   This is ex-detective Ditko calling to report
>   a multiple homicide at Colonel Ames'
>   hacienda. Looks like the Police Commissioner
>   went on a rampage up here, killed the Colonel
>   and a bunch of Tucson's finest citizens.
>   It's a tragedy, boys. Whoever gets here first,
>   gets the promotion. Adios.

He hangs up the microphone.

SAGUARO ROAD   EXT   DAY

JACK's van cruises through the gates and disappears into the forest.

VAN   EXT   DUSK

JACK drives up the canyon, driving badly, holding the wheel between his wounded hands. ERIBERTO and LUIS sit beside him.

CANYON   EXT   DUSK

Everything is unnaturally quiet. The CHILDREN and the CAMP are gone.

JACK gets out. He looks around.

For the first time, we see FEAR in his face.

SUDDENLY the CHILDREN burst from the creek bed and the trees, running at them, shouting.

RUBY follows the KIDS.

>   JACK
>   I've got to tell you something.

                    RUBY
              I already know.

                    JACK
                  (to all)
              We'll make a start first thing tomorrow.

                    CHILDREN
              No! Vamos ahorita, Panchito!
              Ahorita mismo! VAMONOS!

JACK looks at RUBY. RUBY nods.

JACK's legs give out and he collapses. The KIDS drag him towards the van.

LUIS marches up to RUBY.

                    LUIS
                  (in Spanish)
              What about if I drive?

<u>NACO</u>   EXT   NIGHT

The CHOLO VAN cruises towards the border.

On the American side, CUSTOMS OFFICIALS are taking apart a car.

On the Mexican side, a lone BORDER GUARD waves them through.

JACK is sleeping. RUBY drives.

The van's tail light disappears into the night.

                    THE END